laurie polich

STUDIES ON THE GO

Youth Specialties .com

ZONDERVAN.com/
AUTHORTRACKER
follow your favorite authors

Studies on the Go: John
Copyright © 2006 by Laurie Polich

Youth Specialties products, 300 S. Pierce St., El Cajon, CA 92020 are published by Zondervan, 5300 Patterson Ave. SE, Grand Rapids, MI 49530.

Library of Congress Cataloging-in-Publication Data

Polich, Laurie.
Studies on the go : John / by Laurie Polich
p. cm.
ISBN-10: 0-310-27200-9
ISBN-13: 978-0-310-27200-7
1. Bible. N.T. John—Study and teaching. I. Title.
BS2616.P65 2006
266.50071—dc22

2006020460

This edition printed on acid-free paper.

All Scripture quotations, unless otherwise indicated, are taken from the *Holy Bible: New International Version*®. NIV®. Copyright © 1973, 1978, 1984 by International Bible Society. Used by permission of Zondervan. All rights reserved.

All rights reserved. No part of this publication may be reproduced, stored in a retrieval system, or transmitted in any form or by any means—electronic, mechanical, photocopy, recording, or any other—except for brief quotations in printed reviews, without the prior permission of the publisher.

Creative Team: Dave Urbanski, Erika Hueneke, Anna Hammond, Brad Taylor, and SharpSeven
Cover Design by Toolbox Studios

Printed in the United States of America

06 07 08 09 10 11 12 • 20 19 18 17 16 15 14 13 12 11 10 9 8 7 6 5 4 3 2 1

PRAISE FOR *STUDIES ON THE GO*

"Laurie Polich knows how to communicate life-transforming, biblical truth in such a practical way. With Studies on the Go she gets students talking and feeling comfortable, as well as helping them think, learn, and apply Scripture to everyday life. These Bible studies are outstanding."
—Jim Burns, Ph.D., president of HomeWord; author of *Creating an Intimate Marriage*

"Laurie has always been the master of small group discussion questions. This time she has outdone herself. Students are able to allow the passage to speak to their hearts and minds. Anyone considering leading a group through the Gospel of John must have this book."
—*Les Christie, chair, Youth Ministry Department, William Jessup University*

"Laurie has taken the rich truths woven through John and made them accessible, understandable, and practical. Her insightful questions make this a perfect guide for group discussion or personal quiet times. If you want to introduce your students to Jesus, this guide will give them a great picture of who he is."
—*Dr. Marv Penner, Briercrest College and Seminary, Caronport, Saskatchewan, Canada; author of Help! My Kids Are Hurting*

"This is 'drive the truth home' curriculum that will engage your students by using one of Jesus' favorite teaching techniques: asking good, honest, penetrating, practical questions. Laurie has given us a resource that reflects her love for Scripture, her respect for teenagers, and her trust in God to speak through his Word. I highly recommend it."
—*Duffy Robbins, author of This Way to Youth Ministry; Professor of Youth Ministry, Eastern University, St. Davids, Pennsylvania*

DEDICATION

To the staff and community of Ocean Hills Covenant Church—I am grateful that God led me to Santa Barbara to do life and ministry with you.

ACKNOWLEDGEMENTS

Tic Long and Mark Oestreicher: Thanks for 14 years of incredible ministry and memories on the Youth Specialties Core Team.

Jon Ireland: Thanks for your leadership and support in this new chapter of ministry.

Jay Howver: Thanks for helping me bring this idea to print. Hope for more studies to come!

Dave Urbanski: Thanks for being a tireless and patient editor.

CONTENTS

INTRODUCTION

This book is called *Studies on the Go*. Maybe it should have been titled, "Studies for People on the Go." Don't presume these Bible studies are superficial. These 30 studies are filled with questions that are anything but.

Questions have the power to change people. That's what makes them so important. Through his questions, Jesus inspired people to receive healing they didn't know they needed, confront struggles they didn't know they had, and expose secrets they didn't know they kept. And Jesus invites us to that same ministry today. That's what makes your partnership with this book so exciting.

With *Studies on the Go*, you'll be armed with all the questions you need to lead 30 studies through the book of John. Your students will not only gain a solid grasp of this book of the Bible, but also they'll have a better understanding of how it applies to their lives. That's the real goal of Bible study.

You'll notice three kinds of questions in these studies—Observation, Interpretation, and Application. Observation questions take your students *to* the text (their answers come from the Scripture). Interpretation questions lead your students *through* the text (their answers come from what their brains are telling them about the Scripture). Application questions help your students *live* the text (their answers come from how they apply the Scripture). Each study is prefaced by a short introduction that gives shape and form and context to the study. The sessions begin with sharing questions (designed to break the ice) and end with group exercises (designed to bring the lesson home). There are also reproducible quiet time sheets after each study for students who want to dig deeper into the session on their own. (As always, do what suits your group and your schedule the best; you don't have to use every question in the book, and you can feel free to add to them or alter them.)

So that's a brief tour of *Studies on the Go*. Enjoy this ministry tool, and remember—your Savior did his finest work through his questions. Perhaps you will, too!

1. LETTING GOD SHINE

John 1:1-34

Overview: The first 18 verses of the Gospel of John are a bit like the beginning of a musical, where the orchestra plays an overture of the songs will be heard throughout the show. Here John introduces the themes of his Gospel, and he will explain and emphasize each theme as the Gospel progresses. The first theme to unfold is the role of John the Baptist.

We find perhaps the best synopsis of John's ministry in verse 7: "He came as a witness to testify concerning that light, so that *through* him all men might believe" (emphasis added). Many Israelites believed *in* John and his ministry, but instead he led them to believe *through* him—so that they directed their belief toward Christ.

John the Baptist is the prime model of a witness to all believers—setting the example that *through* us we always point people *to* Jesus. This session will reveal how.

SHARE

Warm-Up Qs (*use one or more as needed depending on your group*)

1. What do an understudy, best man, and maid of honor have in common?
2. Have you ever been second place? Was the experience good or bad? Why?
3. Have you ever had a good friend who was better than you at something? Without naming names, how did (does) it affect your friendship?

OBSERVE

Observation Qs

4. Read John 1:1-9. How is Jesus introduced in this passage? How is John introduced? What is the difference between them?
5. What was John's purpose for coming to this earth? (v. 7) Who sent him? (v. 6)
6. Read vv. 15-28. What does John say about Jesus in v. 15? What does he say about himself?
7. What does John the Baptist say to the priests and Levites in v. 20? What do they ask him next? How does John finally respond in v. 23?

THINK

Interpretation Qs

8. Read vv. 8, 15, and 20. Based on these verses, do you think people believe that John is greater than Jesus? Why or why not?
9. Look at vv. 19-27. Which of the following words best describes John the Baptist? *Strong Weak Humble Conceited Strange Insecure* What ideas in the passage led you to choose the word(s) you did?
10. Look ahead at John 3:28-30. Based on what you've read in chapter 1 so far, why do you think John uses the illustration in

this passage to describe his relationship to Jesus and role in the gospel story?

11. How do you think John felt about his role? Do you think he envied Jesus? Why or why not?

APPLY

Application Qs

12. How is John the Baptist a role model for us? What do we learn from him?
13. On a scale of 1–10, how good are you at letting other people shine? Can you be happy for others, or are you bothered when others get attention?

    1 2 3 4 5 6 7 8 9 10

    Bothered by others' success — Happy for others' success

14. How good are you at letting God shine? Do you feel like you point people to God with the things you say and do? Why or why not?
15. What's one thing you can do this week to point someone to God?

DO

Optional Activity: In this session John the Baptist is a signpost, pointing people to God. While he attracts attention with his words and life, he leads people to turn their attention to Jesus. If you made a sign that represented you as a Christian, what would it look like? Would it be big and obvious? Small and subtle? What words would be on it? Any pictures? Draw a sign that best describes you as a Christian and share it with your group.

Day 1: John 1:1-5

1. What word or phrase stands out to you from this passage? Why?
2. How is this passage similar to Genesis 1:1? How is it different?
3. Spend time today thinking about how you have experienced life and/or light in your relationship with Christ.

Day 2: John 1:6-9

1. What word or phrase stands out to you from this passage? Why?
2. What was John's purpose here on earth? How is it similar to ours?
3. Spend time today thinking about how you have been a witness to the light of Christ.

Day 3: John 1:10-14

1. What word or phrase stands out to you from this passage? Why?
2. According to this passage, how do we become children of God? Have you become a child of God?
3. Spend time today thinking about being God's child and what it means to you.

Day 4: John 1:15-18

1. What word or phrase stands out to you from this passage? Why?
2. How could Jesus have come before John if Jesus was born after John? What do you think this means?
3. Spend time today thinking about what we learn about God (and how we view God) through Jesus.

Day 5: John 1:19-28

1. What word or phrase stands out to you from this passage? Why?
2. Who do people think John is? Who does John say he is?
3. Spend time today thinking about John's resolve to carry out his mission, and how it's an example to us.

Day 6: John 1:29-34

1. What word or phrase stands out to you from this passage? Why?
2. What does John call Jesus? Why do you think he refers to Jesus in this way?
3. Spend time today thinking about how Jesus takes away your sin and gives you new life.

Day 7: John 1:1-34

Read through the whole passage and write out the verse that spoke to you the most this week. Meditate on that verse today—and for an extra challenge, memorize it!

From *Studies on the Go* by Laurie Polich. Permission granted to reproduce this page for use in buyer's youth group only. Copyright 2006, Youth Specialties.

2. FOLLOW ME

John 1:35-51

Overview: In this passage Jesus meets his disciples for the first time. He tells them, "Follow me." He doesn't give them a map or a schedule. He doesn't consult them about their plans. Instead he invites them to become a part of *his* schedule and conform themselves to *his* plans. That's what it means to be a follower of Jesus Christ.

The disciples in this passage come to Jesus in different ways. Andrew had been a follower of John the Baptist, but John points Andrew toward Jesus. Andrew brings his brother Simon (Peter). Philip meets Jesus and decides to follow him on the spot. Nathanael is drawn by Jesus' personal touch. Looking at these stories, your students will recount their own stories of how they came to know Jesus. And it will help them consider how closely they are following him now. When Jesus says, "Follow me," he's telling us to put our lives in his hands. Those willing to take this risk will "lose" their lives. But that's ultimately how they'll find their lives.

SHARE

Warm-Up Qs

1. Have you ever met someone you felt a connection with immediately? What was it that made you feel that connection? Did you end up becoming friends?
2. Would you consider yourself more of a leader or a follower? Why?
3. Have you ever given up something you had once joined because it got too hard (e.g., sports team, health club, accountability group, etc.)? What made you quit? Do you ever regret it?

OBSERVE

Observation Qs

4. Read John 1:35-39. Who were the first two disciples of Jesus originally following? Why do they decide to follow Jesus instead?
5. What does Jesus ask the first two followers? What does he eventually invite them to do? (v. 39)
6. How does Simon Peter end up following Jesus? (vv. 40-42) What does Jesus say to him? (v. 42)
7. Read vv. 43-49. What's the difference between how Jesus approaches Philip and Nathanael? What does Jesus say that convinces Nathanael to follow him?

THINK

Interpretation Qs

8. Why do you suppose Jesus asks the first two disciples what they want? (v. 38) Does that seem like a cold thing to say? Why or why not?
9. How do you think Simon Peter felt when Jesus gave him a new name? (v. 42) Why do you think Jesus did this?
10. Look at what Jesus says to Nathanael in v. 47. Why does Jesus say this? (vv. 45-46) Based on Nathanael's response in v. 48, how do you think this made Nathanael feel?

11. Look at what Nathanael says in v. 49. Does it seem like an extreme thing to say? Why or why not?

APPLY

Application Qs

12. Of all the disciples who decide to follow Jesus in John 1:35-49, to whom do you relate the most—and why?
    A. Andrew, who was following someone else before Jesus (v. 40)
    B. Simon Peter, who was brought by his brother to follow Jesus (vv. 41-42)
    C. Philip, who decides to follow Jesus on the spot (v. 43)
    D. Nathanael, who was skeptical at first, but was soon convinced (vv. 46-49)
13. What does it mean to follow Jesus today? Is it the same now as it was then? Do you consider yourself a follower of Jesus?
14. As you look at Jesus' words in vv. 50-51, what are the "greater things" Jesus is talking about? Can you think of things that are greater than what the disciples saw here?
15. If you are a follower of Jesus, how do you follow him? Are you right behind him? Far behind him? Do you ever try to be in front of him (so you can have control)?

DO

Optional Activity: On a piece of paper, draw a cross. Put an X on the page where you see yourself in your walk with Jesus (ahead of him, next to him, behind him, way behind him, off the page, etc.). Tell your group why you drew yourself where you did.

Day 1: John 1:35-36

1. What word or phrase stands out to you from these verses? Why?
2. How does John take the attention off himself and place it on Jesus?
3. Spend time today thinking about how you can take the attention off yourself and point to Jesus.

Day 2: John 1:37-39

1. What word or phrase stands out to you from this passage? Why?
2. Why do you think the disciples started following Jesus? Are you following him?
3. Spend time today thinking about how you can follow Jesus more closely in your day-to-day life.

Day 3: John 1:40-42

1. What word or phrase stands out to you from this passage? Why?
2. What's the first thing Andrew does when he begins following Jesus?
3. Spend time today thinking about whom to invite to have a relationship with Jesus. How will you take steps toward this?

Day 4: John 1:43-46

1. What word or phrase stands out to you from this passage? Why?
2. How do Philip's actions compare to Andrew's actions in v. 41?
3. Spend time today thinking about how God wants to use you in the lives of your friends.

Day 5: John 1:47-48

1. What word or phrase stands out to you from these verses? Why?
2. Do you think Jesus knows you the way he knows Nathanael? Why or why not?
3. Spend time today thinking about how well God knows you—and how that makes you feel.

Day 6: John 1:49-51

1. What word or phrase stands out to you from this passage? Why?
2. What causes Nathanael to believe Jesus is the Son of God? How does Jesus respond?
3. Spend time today thinking about what caused you to believe that Jesus is truly God's Son.

Day 7: John 1:35-51

Read through the whole passage and write out the verse that spoke to you the most this week. Meditate on that verse today—and for an extra challenge, memorize it!

From *Studies on the Go* by Laurie Polich. Permission granted to reproduce this page for use in buyer's youth group only. Copyright 2006, Youth Specialties.

3. LIFE OF THE PARTY

John 2:1-12

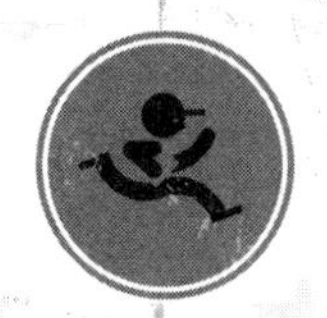

Overview: Imagine Jesus at a party. Where do you picture him? Probably the last place you'd imagine is by the sink, quietly changing the tap water into fine wine. But that's basically where we find him in this passage.

Here we see a side of Jesus that surprises many Christians. But it's not just about Jesus turning water into wine—it's about the *kind* of wine Jesus provides.

The party guests are happy with their less-superior wine because they never had anything better. Your students may find themselves in that same boat. Our culture tells them they will find fulfillment in food, alcohol, money, and sex. But these things only satisfy for a while—and if they keep indulging, they're left feeling emptier than before. Like the wedding host says in this passage, the wine—or satisfaction we try to provide for ourselves—may seem choice at first, but it usually tastes cheap in the end. Only the wine Jesus provides gets better with time.

SHARE

Warm-Up Qs

1. What makes a party successful? What makes people want to stay? What might make them want to leave?
2. If you were going to throw a party with your friends, and you had the opportunity to have Jesus there, do you think the party would be more fun or less fun? Why?
3. What are some things that give us immediate pleasure? Of all those things, which do you enjoy most?

OBSERVE

Observation Qs

4. Read John 2:1-4. What does Mary say to Jesus? What is his response? (v. 4) Based on Jesus' words, what does it seem like Jesus is going to do?
5. Look at what happens in vv. 5-7. What makes Jesus get involved in this dilemma? Based on these verses, what observations do you make about Mary and Jesus' relationship?
6. Read vv. 7-10. What does Jesus tell the servants to do? What does the master of the banquet say? (v. 10)
7. Look at v. 11. How many miracles had Jesus performed before this? What happens as a result of this miracle?

THINK

Interpretation Qs

8. Why do you think Mary tells Jesus they had run out of wine? Do you think she knew he could do something about it? Why or why not?
9. What do you think Jesus means in v. 4 when he says, "My time has not yet come"?

10. How do you think the servants felt when Jesus had them draw water they poured and take it to the master of the banquet? (v. 8) How do you think they felt after the master tasted it? (v. 9)
11. Look at what the master says in v. 10. How is Jesus' wine different from the wine normally served at this point in the party? What does that tell you about Jesus?

APPLY

Application Qs

12. If you were at a party with Jesus and they ran out of wine, would you tell him? Why or why not?
13. Does it surprise you that this is Jesus' first miracle? How does it change your concept of him?
14. Do you think it's significant that the wine Jesus makes is the best wine at the party? Why or why not?
15. Is this a story you would tell your friends? Do you think they'd be drawn to Jesus after hearing it or turned off? Is there someone you could tell it to this week?

DO

Optional Activity: Have two people in the group role-play a Christian telling this story to a nonbeliever. How would you explain Jesus' actions in this story? How would you explain his motives? What does Jesus reveal about himself through this story?

Day 1: John 2:1-3

1. What word or phrase stands out to you from this passage? Why?
2. Why do you think Jesus' mother told him about the wine?
3. Spend time today thinking about some of the issues or problems in your life and whether or not you take them to Jesus first.

Day 2: John 2:4-5

1. What word or phrase stands out to you from these verses? Why?
2. Why does Jesus say his time has not yet come? What does he mean?
3. Spend time today thinking about God's timing in your life: Is there anything for which you are asking him that's not happening in your timing?

Day 3: John 2:6-8

1. What word or phrase stands out to you from this passage? Why?
2. How do you think the servants felt when Jesus told them what to do?
3. Spend time today thinking about what ways God may be asking you to step out in faith.

Day 4: John 2:9

1. What word or phrase stands out to you from this verse? Why?
2. Who knows what's going on here? Who doesn't?
3. Spend time today thinking about how God may be working in ways you don't realize.

Day 5: John 2:10

1. What word or phrase stands out to you from this verse? Why?
2. How does the wine Jesus makes compare to the other wine the guests are drinking?
3. Spend time today thinking about the ways Jesus satisfies us compared to the ways we try to seek satisfaction.

Day 6: John 2:11-12

1. What word or phrase stands out to you from these verses? Why?
2. Does it surprise you that turning water into wine is Jesus' first miracle?
3. Spend time today thinking about the ways God surprises us—and how you can be open to his surprises in your life.

Day 7: John 2:1-12

Read through the whole passage and write out the verse that spoke to you the most this week. Meditate on that verse today—and for an extra challenge, memorize it!

From *Studies on the Go* by Laurie Polich. Permission granted to reproduce this page for use in buyer's youth group only. Copyright 2006, Youth Specialties.

4. CLEANING HOUSE

John 2:13-25

Overview: Any of your students who picture Jesus in a white robe, picking flowers and skipping along the shores of Galilee will find this passage a bit disruptive. Cracking his whip and knocking down tables, Jesus shows us that some things make him really mad. And misusing God's house is one of them.

This still happens today. People do things "in the name of Jesus" that are really for personal gain. Whether someone uses the church to build an income or an image, God is not pleased. Many "strong" Christians allow their passion for honoring God to become a drive for money and power instead. Eventually they (and the people around them) suffer for their sin. This story is a warning not to head down that path.

From Jesus' behavior in this passage, your students will learn an important lesson: The only thing we should worship in God's house is God.

SHARE

Warm-Up Qs

1. What's one thing that makes you really mad?
2. When was the last time you saw someone lose his or her temper? Do you think that person's behavior was appropriate or inappropriate? Why?
3. Have you ever witnessed (or heard about) someone abusing power or money in the name of religion? If so, how did it make you feel?

OBSERVE

Observation Qs

4. Read John 2:13-17. What time of year does Jesus go up to the temple in Jerusalem? What does he find when he arrives?
5. How does Jesus respond to what he sees in the temple? What does he say? What does he do? What observation do the disciples make?
6. Read vv. 18-25. What question do the Jews ask Jesus in response to his actions? How does Jesus respond? How do the disciples interpret his statement later on? (v. 22)
7. Look at vv. 23-25. How do the people respond to Jesus' miracles? What does v. 25 say about Jesus' response?

THINK

Interpretation Qs

8. Does Jesus' response to the moneychangers surprise you? (vv. 15-16) Why or why not? Is Jesus' behavior consistent with what you know about him?
9. Look at the exchange between the Jews and Jesus in vv. 18-20. Do you think they were looking for evidence to believe in him or to condemn him? Why?

10. Look at Jesus' statement in v. 19. When do the disciples fully understand what Jesus said? (vv. 21-22) Does that tell you anything about the way God works in our lives?
11. Why do you think Jesus would not "entrust himself" to people? (v. 24) Do you understand his reasoning in v. 25? Do you agree with him?

APPLY

Application Qs

12. How does this passage affect your impression of Jesus? Are you surprised by his behavior? Why or why not?
13. If Jesus were to walk into your church, which of the following emotions would he feel?
    - A. Right at home—excited about your ministry
    - B. A little bored—wishing there was more life
    - C. Upset and angry—sensing your church was not on the right track
14. What (do you think) makes Jesus angry today? Are there things Christians do that anger him? If so, what?
15. Can you think of a situation or circumstance to which Christians should respond with anger? Is there anything that makes you angry as a Christian?

DO

Optional Activity: As a group, think of something specific you can do this week to express your anger in a positive way (e.g., anger about world hunger = sponsor a child; anger about homelessness = volunteer in a shelter; anger about abortion = help someone who's pregnant). Choose one thing and decide how you will act on it, either individually or as a group.

Day 1: John 2:13-14

1. What word or phrase stands out to you from these verses? Why?
2. How do you think Jesus must have felt when he saw what was going on in the temple?
3. Spend time today thinking about what the church should be used for—and what it *shouldn't* be used for.

Day 2: John 2:15-17

1. What word or phrase stands out to you from this passage? Why?
2. Does Jesus' reaction to what he sees at the temple surprise you? Why or why not?
3. Spend time today thinking about what might anger Jesus in today's culture.

Day 3: John 2:18-19

1. What word or phrase stands out to you from these verses? Why?
2. How do you think the Jews felt when Jesus said what he did? How would you have felt?
3. Spend time today thinking about the words Jesus says that can be confusing when you first hear them but make sense later on.

Day 4: John 2:20-21

1. What word or phrase stands out to you from these verses? Why?
2. How do the Jews misunderstand Jesus by taking him literally? Have you ever done this?
3. Spend time today thinking about things Jesus says that are figures of speech and are used to make a larger point.

Day 5: John 2:22

1. What word or phrase stands out to you from this verse? Why?
2. How were Jesus' words interpreted differently in time? What does that tell you about how to interpret him?
3. Spend time today thinking about the things Jesus did that were understood differently when people looked back.

Day 6: John 2:23-25

1. What word or phrase stands out to you from this passage? Why?
2. According to these verses, do you think Jesus cares about what people think of him? Why or why not?
3. Spend time today thinking about how we can follow Jesus' example in regard to how we respond to what people think or say about us.

Day 7: John 2:13-25

Read through the whole passage and write out the verse that spoke to you the most this week. Meditate on that verse today—and for an extra challenge, memorize it!

From *Studies on the Go* by Laurie Polich. Permission granted to reproduce this page for use in buyer's youth group only. Copyright 2006, Youth Specialties.

5. SECOND BIRTH

John 3:1-21

Overview: It's safe to say most people would describe Nicodemus as a person who knew God—except maybe Nicodemus. That's why he came to Jesus in this passage. Through this conversation with Jesus, Nicodemus discovers there is a difference between knowing *about* God and knowing God. It's a humbling lesson for him to learn. Nicodemus finds out that no matter how much knowledge he has about God, in order to truly know God, he must be born again. Becoming a Christian can happen no other way.

In this session your students will discover what Jesus means when he says we must be "born again." Perhaps no other biblical phrase is so widely misunderstood, yet it's immensely important to understanding the Christian faith. It's the way we begin a relationship with God—and no amount of effort or even religious standing can ever achieve that relationship. As John 3:16 states, we receive it as a gift. God has done all the work. Our job is to respond with faith.

SHARE
Warm-Up Qs

1. If you could have a one-on-one conversation with God on any topic, what would you talk to him about? Is there a particular question you would ask? If so, what?
2. When you hear the words *born again,* what do you think about? Do these words have a positive or negative connotation to you? To others? Why?
3. If you had the choice of conversing with God in private or with a group of friends, which would you choose? Why?

OBSERVE
Observation Qs

4. Read John 3:1-8. Who was Nicodemus? When did he come to Jesus? What does he say to him?
5. What is the first thing Jesus says to Nicodemus? (v. 3) Was it in response to a question? How does Nicodemus respond? (v. 4)
6. How does Jesus describe being born again? (vv. 5-8) What image does he use to describe the spirit's work? (v. 8)
7. Read vv. 16-21. What motivated God to send his Son to us? (v. 16) What happens to people who believe in Jesus? (v. 18) What happens to people who don't?

THINK
Interpretation Qs

8. Look at Jesus' first words to Nicodemus in v. 3. Why do you think Jesus said these words to him? Do you think Nicodemus understood? Why or why not?
9. In vv. 5-8, Jesus compares being born of the Spirit to the wind. Why do you think he does this? How is the work of the Spirit similar to the work of the wind?

10. What tone does Jesus use with Nicodemus in v. 10? Why do you think he spoke to him this way? Is he talking just to Nicodemus or to the Pharisees in general? (v. 11)
11. In vv. 16-21, Jesus gives perhaps the best explanation of what it means to be a Christian. Have each person in your group take one verse from this passage and explain, in his or her own words, what each verse means.

APPLY

Application Qs

12. If someone asked you how to become a Christian, what would you say?
13. Would you describe yourself as "born again"? What does that phrase mean to you in your own life?
14. Have you seen evidence of the Spirit's work in your life or in someone else's life? Share an example of how you've seen the Spirit work in you or in people around you.
15. In vv. 19-21 Jesus talks about living in the dark versus living in the light. On a scale of 1–10, 1 being dark and 10 being light, where do you put yourself? Are you where you want to be? If not, what would it take to get there?

DO

Optional Activity: This week make a chart by dividing a page in half, labeling one half "Deeds of Light" and the other "Deeds of Darkness." At the end of each day, chart your conversations, actions, and attitudes, determining if they were light, dark, or neutral. Determine at the end of the week whether you need to work on doing fewer deeds of darkness or more deeds of light.

Day 1: John 3:1-3

1. What word or phrase stands out to you from this passage? Why?
2. Why do you think Nicodemus came to Jesus? Do you think he thought the conversation would start the way it did?
3. Spend time today thinking about the first thing Jesus would say to you if the two of you had a conversation.

Day 2: John 3:4-5

1. What word or phrase stands out to you from these verses? Why?
2. How did Nicodemus misunderstand Jesus? What did Jesus mean when he said "born of water and of the Spirit"?
3. Spend time today thinking about whether or not you have been born of water and of the Spirit. If you are not sure what this means, ask someone!

Day 3: John 3:6-8

1. What word or phrase stands out to you from these verses? Why?
2. How does being born of the Spirit compare to the wind?
3. Spend time today thinking about how we see the effects of being "born again," and whether or not people can see a difference in your life.

Day 4: John 3:9-15

1. What word or phrase stands out to you from this passage? Why?
2. Do you understand what Jesus is saying in this passage? Which words do you understand? Which words don't you understand?
3. Spend time today thinking about how the "lifting up" of Jesus (v. 14) paved the way for us to have eternal life.

Day 5: John 3:16-18

1. What word or phrase stands out to you from this passage? Why?
2. What was God's purpose in sending Christ into the world? What do we need to do to have eternal life?
3. Spend time today thinking about who might need to hear the words of this passage, and how you can share them.

Day 6: John 3:19-21

1. What word or phrase stands out to you from this passage? Why?
2. According to this passage, what does it take to live in the light? What does it mean to live in darkness?
3. Spend time today thinking about how much of your life is lived in light and how much is lived in darkness.

Day 7: John 3:1-21

Read through the whole passage and write out the verse that spoke to you the most this week. Meditate on that verse today—and for an extra challenge, memorize it!

From *Studies on the Go* by Laurie Polich. Permission granted to reproduce this page for use in buyer's youth group only. Copyright 2006, Youth Specialties.

6. THE FIRST MISSIONARY

John 4:1-42

Overview: We all have secrets. The woman in this story does, too. That's why she comes to get water in the middle of the day. She chooses a time when no one is there so she can do her business and slip out of sight. But her plan is ruined when she runs into Jesus.

This woman has tried to find love in all the wrong places. Some of your students will relate. Because of her choices, she lives in shame and isolation. But after this encounter with Jesus, she's never the same.

Jesus offers her living water—but he exposes her secrets first. Through gentle questioning Jesus helps this woman recognize her thirst so she can receive the true satisfaction her heart craves. A new woman emerges from this encounter, and this once-isolated person becomes the first missionary, shouting her testimony to all who will listen.

Through this lesson your students will learn that our secrets keep us from God—but they don't keep God from us. And with his help, our shame can become our testimony.

SHARE

Warm-Up Qs

1. Where do you go when you want to be alone? When was the last time you went there?
2. Who's the last person you'd expect to start a conversation with you? Why would it surprise you?
3. How do you feel when someone you don't know asks you a personal question? Have you ever had a personal discussion with someone you didn't know very well?

OBSERVE

Observation Qs

4. Read John 4:1-10. What time is it when Jesus arrives at the well in Samaria? Whom does he speak to? Who initiates the conversation?
5. What's the first thing the Samaritan woman says to Jesus? (v. 9) Does he answer her question? What does he say in response to her?
6. Read vv. 11-18. What kind of water does Jesus offer this woman? How does he describe it? (vv. 13-14) What does he ask the woman to do when she asks for the water? How does she respond?
7. Read vv. 19-26. What does Jesus say about worship in this passage? Does it matter where we worship? What matters most about our worship, according to Jesus? (vv. 23-24)

THINK

Interpretation Qs

8. Look at vv. 9-10. Do you think it mattered to Jesus that this woman is a Samaritan? As you look at his response, what do you think matters most to Jesus?

9. What do you think Jesus means when he offers the woman living water? (vv. 13-14) Is he being literal or symbolic? What does he want before he gives her the water? (vv. 16-18)
10. Does Jesus' conversation with the woman in vv. 16-18 relate to his definition of true worship? (v. 23) If so, how?
11. Look at vv. 28-42. How do we see evidence that this woman's encounter with Jesus changes her? Is her behavior here different from her behavior at the beginning of the chapter? If so, how? (Have your group point out specific differences.)

APPLY

Application Qs

12. If you met Jesus at a well and it was just the two of you, what do you think he'd say? Would he ask you to do something? If so, what?
13. Have you ever experienced the "living water" Jesus describes in this passage? If so, how? If not, what do you think it might be like?
14. Has your life ever been changed because of an encounter with Jesus? (Try to think of a specific example.) If not, how might your life be different today if you were to encounter him?
15. Look at the woman's testimony in v. 39. If you were to share your experience with God in one or two sentences, what would your testimony be?

DO

Optional Activity: Have your group spend the week writing their personal testimonies. Encourage them to fit their individual stories into a half-page or less. Have your students bring them next week to share with the group. (You can have one person share each week or designate a small group time just for this.)

Day 1: John 4:1-9

1. What word or phrase stands out to you from this passage? Why?
2. Why is the woman surprised that Jesus initiates a conversation with her? Do you think Jesus cares about the things she thinks would be a barrier?
3. Spend time today thinking about how God goes the extra mile to find us—even when we're not looking for him.

Day 2: John 4:10-15

1. What word or phrase stands out to you from this passage? Why?
2. What kind of water does Jesus offer the woman? Do you think she understood what he was talking about?
3. Spend time today thinking about the kind of water Jesus offers us and how it satisfies us compared to the things we use to try to quench our thirst.

Day 3: John 3:16-19

1. What word or phrase stands out to you from this passage? Why?
2. Why does Jesus tell the woman to go call her husband? Is he just being mean? Why or why not?
3. Spend time today thinking about what Jesus would confront you about if he had a heart-to-heart talk with you.

Day 4: John 4:20-26

1. What word or phrase stands out to you from this passage? Why?
2. What does Jesus say about true worshipers? Is it important where they worship or how they worship?
3. Spend time today thinking about how you worship and whether or not you're being truthful before God.

Day 5: John 4:27-30

1. What word or phrase stands out to you from this passage? Why?
2. What changes do you see in this woman after her encounter with Jesus?
3. Spend time today thinking about how you've changed because of your relationship with Jesus, and how you can share those changes with others.

Day 6: John 4:39-42

1. What word or phrase stands out to you from this passage? Why?
2. How does the woman help the Samaritans believe in Jesus? Do they ultimately believe because of her—or because of Jesus?
3. Spend time today thinking about who first told you about his or her relationship with Jesus and how you came to know Jesus yourself.

Day 7: John 4:1-42

Read through the whole passage and write out the verse that spoke to you the most this week. Meditate on that verse today—and for an extra challenge, memorize it!

From *Studies on the Go* by Laurie Polich. Permission granted to reproduce this page for use in buyer's youth group only. Copyright 2006, Youth Specialties.

7. POWER TO HEAL

John 4:43–5:15

Overview: Often our prayers are consumed with asking God to change our circumstances. But God is involved in a more important agenda—changing us.

In this passage are two different stories of healing, and they illustrate the different ways God works in our lives. The first man takes the initiative and asks Jesus for healing; the second man is asked by Jesus if he wants to be healed. Their encounters with Jesus challenge both of them to take the next step in their faith—and each of their healings is connected to their response.

Jesus tells the first man to go home. He must believe Jesus for something he can't see. Jesus tells the second man to get up. He must believe Jesus for something he can't do. As they respond to the words of Jesus, they receive their healing. In these stories your students will discover that God works in our lives by meeting us where we are—and taking us where we've never been. That is the journey of faith.

SHARE

Warm-Up Qs

1. When you get sick, is your first tendency to pray, call a doctor, or talk to your parents? Why?
2. Do you think God has the power to heal people? If so, why doesn't he always exercise it?
3. Have you ever prayed for healing (for you or someone else)? If so, what happened?

OBSERVE

Observation Qs

4. Read John 4:43-54. What is Jesus' response to the man who begs him to heal his son? (v. 48) How does his response change in v. 50?
5. How does the man respond to Jesus' promise of healing? (v. 50) What does he find out on the way home? (vv. 51-53) What result does the healing have on his household?
6. Read John 5:1-15. What's the first question Jesus asks the man by the pool? (v. 6) Does the man respond by answering the question? What does he say? (v. 7) How does Jesus respond to him? (v. 8)
7. How long does it take for the man to be healed? (v. 9) When does the healing take place? (vv. 9-10) What does Jesus say to the man when he sees him again? (v. 14)

THINK

Interpretation Qs

8. What's the difference between the way Jesus heals in John 4 and the way he heals in John 5? What (if anything) does that tell you about the way Jesus heals people?
9. Are there any similarities between the two men Jesus encounters in these two passages? What are the differences? Who do you think has more faith? Why?

10. Why do you think Jesus asked the man in John 5:6 if he wanted to get well? Do you think it was obvious—or not? What does the man reveal about himself in v. 7?
11. Why would Jesus say what he says v. 14? Do you think it's worse to be physically sick or spiritually sick? Why?

APPLY

Application Qs

12. Whose situation do you relate to more—the man who asks for healing in John 4 or the man who's healed without asking in John 5? Why?
13. Which of the two men are you most like?
14. Have you ever been afraid to ask God for healing? If so, why? If not, why not?
15. If you could ask God to heal anything and you knew he would do it, what would you ask him to do? How would your life change because of that healing?

DO

Optional Activity: Pass out index cards and have each person write down one thing for which he or she would like healing. Fold the index cards, put them in the middle, and have everyone pick a card. During the following week, have each person pray for the requests on the cards they picked up.

Day 1: John 4:43-48

1. What word or phrase stands out to you from this passage? Why?
2. Why does Jesus respond the way he does to the man's request? Do you think he was testing him?
3. Spend time today thinking about whether you need God to act in certain ways in order to trust him.

Day 2: John 4:49-50

1. What word or phrase stands out to you from these verses? Why?
2. How does the man show his faith in Jesus? Could you have responded this way?
3. Spend time today thinking about whether or not you can take Jesus at his word.

Day 3: John 4:51-54

1. What word or phrase stands out to you from this passage? Why?
2. What caused the man's household to believe? Do you think the man's faith played a part in their belief?
3. Spend time today thinking about whether or not your faith is a testimony to others.

Day 4: John 5:1-6

1. What word or phrase stands out to you from this passage? Why?
2. Why do you think Jesus asked the man if he wanted to get well if he was lying by a healing pool?
3. Spend time today thinking about the times you aren't willing to step out in faith and receive the healing you need.

Day 5: John 5:7-9

1. What word or phrase stands out to you from this passage? Why?
2. How does Jesus respond to the man's excuses? How do you think he responds to your excuses?
3. Spend time today thinking about the things for which you need to stop making excuses and instead respond to what God's asking you to do.

Day 6: John 5:10-15

1. What word or phrase stands out to you from this passage? Why?
2. What does Jesus say to the man when he sees him again? Why do you think he said this?
3. Spend time today thinking about how sin eventually creates negative consequences in our lives. Is there an area of your life in which this has happened?

Day 7: John 4:43–5:15

Read through the whole passage and write out the verse that spoke to you the most this week. Meditate on that verse today—and for an extra challenge, memorize it!

From *Studies on the Go* by Laurie Polich. Permission granted to reproduce this page for use in buyer's youth group only. Copyright 2006, Youth Specialties.

8. LIKE FATHER, LIKE SON

John 5:16-47 (also 8:12-30)

Overview: Many call Jesus a great prophet, teacher, and healer. But they stop short of calling him God's Son. This passage makes it clear that in order to accept Jesus, we must accept him as he is—because it's our belief in Jesus as God's Son that leads us to eternal life.

Jesus produces four witnesses that testify to his identity. But many Jews refuse to believe him. As Jesus' claims get bigger and his words get tougher, a line is drawn between those who accept him and those who reject him. The same is true today.

In this session your students will have the opportunity to assess Jesus' claims and determine where they stand in their view of him. This will help clarify where they are in their faith. In this passage Jesus repeatedly alludes to the fact that he is the Son of God. C. S. Lewis writes that Jesus leaves us three choices regarding how we can view him—a lunatic, liar, or Lord.

Your students will decide which.

SHARE
Warm-Up Qs

1. In what ways are you like your father? Do you share any common characteristics? Would people be able to guess that you were his child?
2. Who in your family would you consider "a chip off the old block"—or most like your dad? Why?
3. If someone were to ask you how Jesus and God are connected, what would you say? How are they alike? How are they different?

OBSERVE
Observation Qs

4. Read John 5:16-23. Why are the Jews trying to kill Jesus? What parallels does Jesus draw between himself and God?
5. Read vv. 24-30. What promise does Jesus make in this passage? Who is it for? Is this promise from him or the Father?
6. Read vv. 31-47. According to Jesus, is John's testimony the greatest? Why or why not? Why should the Jews know that Jesus is who he says he is?
7. Now look at John 8:12-30. Name some similarities between the two passages. When does Jesus say people will know that he is who he says he is? (v. 28)

THINK
Interpretation Qs

8. Look at John 5:21-24. According to these verses, how do we receive eternal life? Who makes that decision—God, Jesus, or us?
9. How would you describe Jesus' relationship with the Father?
    A. Separate but close (they function separately and together)

B. Interconnected (they can't function without each other)

What verses in this chapter support your opinion?

10. As you sense Jesus' tone in vv. 39-47, how would you describe his relationship with the Pharisees? Do you think Jesus' words in John 8:19-26 clarified things for the Pharisees or contributed to the tension between them and Jesus?
11. What does Jesus mean when he says in John 5:46 that Moses wrote about him? Does that mean Jesus is in the Old Testament? Do you think that's possible? If so, how?

APPLY

Application Qs

12. If you were there listening to Jesus in this passage, how would you have felt? Do you think you would have been drawn to him or offended by him?
13. Based on this passage, do you think it's possible to believe in God without believing in Jesus? Why or why not?
14. In this passage Jesus gives four testimonies that prove he's God's Son (vv. 33, 36, 37, and 39). Which is most compelling to you? Why?
15. What words best describe your response to Jesus in this passage: Confused, convicted, challenged, or surprised? Why?

DO

Optional Activity: Divide your group in half and stage a debate between Jesus' followers and the Pharisees about whether or not Jesus is the Son of God. Use the arguments in this passage (e.g., Jesus breaking the law by healing on the Sabbath versus Jesus' claim that the Father gives him authority to heal). Have students do research in two groups and then come together for the debate.

Day 1: John 5:16-18

1. What word or phrase stands out to you from this passage? Why?
2. Why do the Jews want to kill Jesus? Why are they so threatened by him?
3. Spend time today thinking about whether or not you're ever threatened by God's authority in your life.

Day 2: John 5:19-23

1. What word or phrase stands out to you from this passage? Why?
2. What do you observe about the Father's relationship with the Son in this passage? How do they work together?
3. Spend time today thinking about how your relationship with Jesus has impacted your relationship with God.

Day 3: John 5:24-25

1. What word or phrase stands out to you from these verses? Why?
2. According to Jesus, what does it take to cross over from death to life? Do we have to do something?
3. Spend time today thinking about whether or not you have the assurance of eternal life. If not, what will give you that assurance?

Day 4: John 5:26-30

1. What word or phrase stands out to you from this passage? Why?
2. Why does Jesus have the authority to judge us? How will we be judged?
3. Spend time today thinking about whether or not you're excited for the day you'll meet Jesus face-to-face.

Day 5: John 5:31-40

1. What word or phrase stands out to you from this passage? Why?
2. What three testimonies does Jesus mention in this passage? Which do you think carries the most weight?
3. Spend time today thinking about whether God, the Bible, or someone else's testimony was the most instrumental in your decision to believe in Jesus.

Day 6: John 5:41-47

1. What word or phrase stands out to you from this passage? Why?
2. What's the difference between praise from people and praise from God? Which of these do you seek most?
3. Spend time today thinking about how you can seek praise from God rather than from the people around you.

Day 7: John 5:16-47

Read through the whole passage and write out the verse that spoke to you the most this week. Meditate on that verse today—and for an extra challenge, memorize it!

From *Studies on the Go* by Laurie Polich. Permission granted to reproduce this page for use in buyer's youth group only. Copyright 2006, Youth Specialties.

9. MIRACLE MAN

John 6:1-24

Overview: In the last session, your students had a chance to hear Jesus' claims. In this session they get to see those claims in action. Jesus begins by feeding more than 5,000 people with two loaves and five fish and then caps off the day with a walk on water. Through these amazing events, people are realizing Jesus' claims are more than just talk. The crowds grow as his reputation spreads.

The feeding of the 5,000 is the only miracle recorded in all four Gospels. But John includes a detail the others leave out—a small boy who gives up his food so Jesus can do this miracle. Someone with so little was used by Jesus to do so much. And that's something your students shouldn't miss.

In the second miracle, Jesus shows that he's not only a God of provision; he's a God of power. Imagine what the disciples are thinking as they witness this event. Suffice it to say, their faith is given a giant boost. Their view of Jesus would never be the same.

After this session, your students' view of Jesus won't, either.

SHARE
Warm-Up Qs

1. Has God (or God's actions) ever surprised you? If so, when?
2. If you could ask God to do any miracle to show his power, what would you ask God to do?
3. When someone shares a miraculous story, do you tend to be skeptical or excited? Why?

OBSERVE
Observation Qs

4. Read John 6:1-15. What question does Jesus ask Philip? (v. 5) Why does Jesus ask him this question? (v. 6) What is Philip's response? (v. 7)
5. What does Jesus do in order to perform this miracle? (v. 11) How do the people respond? (v. 14)
6. Read vv. 16-21. Who is there to witness Jesus' second miracle? How do they respond?
7. Read vv. 22-24. What does the crowd figure out about the way Jesus and his disciples left the scene? Do you think they all left together? What does the crowd do next?

THINK
Interpretation Qs

8. Why do you think Jesus asks the question in v. 5 when he already knows what he's going to do?
9. Do you think Andrew showed more faith than Philip? (vv. 7-9) Why or why not?
10. How does Jesus respond when he thinks the people might make him king? (v. 15) Why do you think he responds this way?
11. How do you think the disciples' view of Jesus changed when they saw him walk on the water? Do you think they wanted to run away from him or follow him even more?

APPLY

Application Qs

12. Has anything happened in your life that caused you to see God in a new way? If so, what?
13. If you saw an overwhelming need, do you think you'd respond more like Philip, Andrew, or the little boy with the loaves and fish? Why?
14. Which of the two miracles in this chapter most impresses you? Why?
15. What do both of these miracles reveal about Jesus? At this point in your life, would you say you're more in need of Jesus' provision or his power? Why?

DO

Optional Activity: Find a Saturday morning when you can take your group to an area where there are homeless or needy people. Give the students $3 each and have them disperse for one hour (in pairs) with the goal of feeding as many people as they can. Have them come back and report on their experiences.

Day 1: John 6:1-4

1. What word or phrase stands out to you from this passage? Why?
2. Why is a great crowd following Jesus? What are they drawn to?
3. Spend time today thinking about the reasons people are drawn to Jesus. What were the reasons you were drawn to him? Have any of those changed?

Day 2: John 6:5-9

1. What word or phrase stands out to you from this passage? Why?
2. Why does Jesus ask them where they can buy bread? What does that tell you about the way Jesus works in our lives?
3. Spend time today thinking about the ways Jesus asks you questions to test your faith. Is there anything he's asking you right now?

Day 3: John 6:10-13

1. What word or phrase stands out to you from this passage? Why?
2. How much food does Jesus have to work with? Who gives it to him? How much do the people have to eat?
3. Spend time today thinking about what Jesus can do with the things you're willing to give him.

Day 4: John 6:14-15

1. What word or phrase stands out to you from these verses? Why?
2. What do the people want to do with Jesus after this event? How does he respond?
3. Spend time today thinking about the kind of king Jesus is and how we reflect his presence in our lives.

Day 5: John 6:16-21

1. What word or phrase stands out to you from this passage? Why?
2. Do you think the disciples' view of Jesus changed after what happened in this passage? Why or why not?
3. Spend time today thinking about any miracles you've seen God do and how they've impacted your relationship with God.

Day 6: John 6:22-24

1. What word or phrase stands out to you from this passage? Why?
2. What clues in this passage indicate something strange happened with Jesus and his disciples?
3. Spend time today thinking about the clues that show God is powerful and almighty even though we can't see him. What clues do you see around you today?

Day 7: John 6:1-24

Read through the whole passage and write out the verse that spoke to you the most this week. Meditate on that verse today—and for an extra challenge, memorize it!

From *Studies on the Go* by Laurie Polich. Permission granted to reproduce this page for use in buyer's youth group only. Copyright 2006, Youth Specialties.

10. BREAD OF LIFE

John 6:25-71

Overview: When the people ask Jesus to produce more bread, he announces that he *is* the bread. This doesn't do much for his popularity. But Jesus doesn't care about being popular; he cares about sharing the truth. Jesus knows the bread people eat will never permanently fill them; they will always hunger for more. And he is the "more" they need.

It's not what people want to hear. Your students will see that the more Jesus talks, the less popular he becomes. This passage shows that people want Jesus on their terms—but Jesus comes on his own terms. He may not be what we *want* him to be, but he always ends up being what we *need* him to be.

Jesus says, "Whoever eats my flesh and drinks my blood has eternal life." (v. 54) The crowd grumbles and walks away. Now the disciples are left with the final question of faith. Will they hold on to Jesus in spite of their feelings of uncertainty? Will we? This session will help your students decide whether or not they can or will follow Jesus—not as the Lord they want him to be, but as the Lord he is.

SHARE

Warm-Up Qs

1. Has there ever been a time when you lost (or almost lost) your faith? If so, when?
2. What is the purpose of communion? Why do we take it?
3. What's the biggest obstacle that keeps people from following God? What is your biggest obstacle?

OBSERVE

Observation Qs

4. Read John 6:25-40. What does Jesus say is the reason people are following him? (v. 26) Where does he say their focus should be instead? (v. 27)
5. What do the people want from Jesus? (v. 30) What's the difference between the bread the people want and the bread Jesus provides? (vv. 33-35)
6. Read vv. 41-52. How do the Jews respond to Jesus' words? (v. 41) What does Jesus say about people's response to him? (v. 44) What are some of the things Jesus says about himself in vv. 46-51?
7. Read vv. 53-70. What does Jesus say we must do to have life? (vv. 53-54) How do the disciples respond? (vv. 60-61) What does Jesus say about who will follow him and who won't? (v. 65)

THINK

Interpretation Qs

8. Do you think vv. 27-29 say we have to work to gain favor with God? Why or why not? What do you think Jesus means?
9. As you read vv. 29-40, do you think "the work God requires" is more about Jesus' actions or ours? What is our part? What is Jesus' part?

10. When Jesus says we must eat his flesh and drink his blood (vv. 53-58), what do you think he means? Is it just about taking communion? What does Jesus do for people who do this?
11. Why do you think some of Jesus' followers turn away after this teaching? (v. 66) Why do Peter and the Twelve stay? (vv. 67-69) Do you think they wanted to leave, too?

APPLY

Application Qs

12. If you had been there to hear the things Jesus says in this passage, would you have continued to follow him? Why or why not?
13. Does this passage change your understanding of what it means to take communion? If so, how?
14. Do you feel the way Peter does in vv. 68-69? Do you think you would stick with God if you didn't understand what he was doing? Has that ever happened to you?
15. When you hear Jesus say that no one comes to him unless the Father has drawn him or her (vv. 44, 65), does it affect the way you think about sharing your faith? Do you think it's still important for us to do? Why or why not?

DO

Optional Activity: If your denomination allows it, have a time of communion with your group. (If not, arrange to sit together when you have communion at church.) Read vv. 51, 54-57 (before or during communion) and spend time in silence, meditating on Jesus' words. Have each person journal or share their thoughts about their experiences.

Day 1: John 6:25-29

1. What word or phrase stands out to you from this passage? Why?
2. What does Jesus warn his followers about? Why do you think he warns them of this?
3. Spend time today thinking about how much you invest in temporary things versus eternal things. What do you consider temporary? What do you consider eternal?

Day 2: John 6:30-40

1. What word or phrase stands out to you from this passage? Why?
2. How do Jesus' words in this passage remind you of what he says about living water in John 4? What do you think Jesus is saying here?
3. Spend time today thinking about the differences between the satisfaction our culture gives us and the satisfaction God gives us. What's the difference?

Day 3: John 6:41-51

1. What word or phrase stands out to you from this passage? Why?
2. What does Jesus say is the reason we're drawn to him? What does that tell you about the way God is at work in people's lives?
3. Spend time today thinking about how God draws people to himself and what our part is in helping make that happen.

Day 4: John 6:52-56

1. What word or phrase stands out to you from this passage? Why?
2. Is Jesus speaking literally in this passage? How do we eat his flesh and drink his blood?
3. Spend time today thinking about instances when you've taken communion and what Jesus says happens at that moment.

Day 5: John 6:57-66

1. What word or phrase stands out to you from this passage? Why?
2. Why do many of Jesus' disciples stop following him? What would you have done?
3. Spend time today thinking about whether you would continue following Jesus if you were disappointed in him.

Day 6: John 6:67-71

1. What word or phrase stands out to you from this passage? Why?
2. Why does Peter say he's going to continue following Jesus?
3. Spend time today thinking about whether your relationship with God is more like Peter's (who stayed) or the disciples' (who left).

Day 7: John 6:25-71

Read through the whole passage and write out the verse that spoke to you the most this week. Meditate on that verse today—and for an extra challenge, memorize it!

From *Studies on the Go* by Laurie Polich. Permission granted to reproduce this page for use in buyer's youth group only. Copyright 2006, Youth Specialties.

11. GOD'S TIMING

John 7:1-43

Overview: The Feast of Tabernacles is about to begin. It's a huge celebration that lasts seven days. Jesus' brothers think Jesus should go to the Feast and do some miracles to win back the crowd. But Jesus decides not to follow their agenda. The only agenda he's committed to is God's.

Jesus arrives midway through the celebration, and on the last day he stands up and speaks, saying, "If anyone is thirsty, let him come to me and drink." (v. 37) At first glance, we might question the timing of his teaching. The Jews had been eating and drinking for seven days. Why didn't he stand up before they had their fill?

But Jesus' timing was perfect. God's timing always is. It's only after we've filled ourselves up with everything we can that we realize we have a deeper thirst. And there's only one person who can quench it. He's the same one who stood up at the Feast of Tabernacles on the seventh day and said, "If anyone is thirsty, let him come to me and drink." Hopefully after this session, your students will know the invitation still stands.

SHARE

Warm-Up Qs

1. Have you ever asked God for something, and it came at a different time than you wanted? If so, what? Is there anything you wish he'd do that he hasn't done yet?
2. Does God generally move slower than you'd like, faster than you'd like, or just at the right time? (Share reasons for your responses.)
3. Do you ever get frustrated that God doesn't show his power more? Why do you think he holds back?

OBSERVE

Observation Qs

4. Read John 7:1-13. What do Jesus' brothers think Jesus should do? (v. 3) What is their reasoning? (v. 4) What is Jesus' response in v. 6, and what does he end up doing? (v. 10)
5. Read vv. 14-18. When does Jesus arrive at the Feast...and what does he do first? (v. 14) What is the Jews' response to his teaching? (v. 15) Where does Jesus say his teaching comes from? (vv. 16-18)
6. Read vv. 25-34. According to v. 30, why aren't the Pharisees able to seize Jesus? What does Jesus say about how long he will be with the people? (v. 33) Where is he going after that?
7. Read vv. 37-43. When does Jesus finally stand up to address the crowd? (v. 37) To whom is he specifically speaking? What does he say they should do? According to vv. 40-43, how do the people respond?

THINK

Interpretation Qs

8. Look at all the references to timing in this passage. (vv. 6, 8, 14, 30, 33, 37). After reading these verses, would you say Jesus' timing is deliberate or random? Why?

9. Why do you think Jesus' brothers wanted him to "go public" with his miracles? (v. 3) Do you think they were concerned for Jesus? Why or why not?
10. Why do you think Jesus waited to address the crowd until the last day of the Feast? (v. 37) Why didn't he do it earlier?
11. If the people had been eating and drinking for seven days, do you think any of them were still thirsty? If so, why? If not, why would Jesus ask those who were still thirsty to come to him?

APPLY

Application Qs

12. Have you ever had the feeling of wanting something more after you got something you wanted? Why do you think we feel that way?
13. Do you think God allows us to be fully satisfied here on earth? Why or why not?
14. Have you ever found God's timing to be better than yours? In what area of your life do you need to trust God's timing?
15. Do you think people today respond to Christ the same way they did in vv. 40-43? Why or why not? Do you think it was different for people who actually lived during his time?

DO

Optional Activity: Invite an older, more mature Christian whom you respect to come to your group and share what he or she has learned about God's timing. Let your group interview this person and ask questions. At the end, pass out cards with Psalm 27:14 printed on one side, and have your students write something about which they need to trust God's timing on the other side. Tell the students to keep their cards.

Day 1: John 7:1-6

1. What word or phrase stands out to you from this passage? Why?
2. Why do Jesus' brothers want him to go to the Feast? Do you think it was more for themselves or Jesus?
3. Spend time today thinking about your motivation for asking God to do something for you. Do you pray primarily for your own good or for God's good?

Day 2: John 7:7-13

1. What word or phrase stands out to you from this passage? Why?
2. How do the crowds in this passage remind you of people today?
3. Spend time today thinking about what you would say about Jesus if you were in this crowd.

Day 3: John 7:14-24

1. What word or phrase stands out to you from this passage? Why?
2. How does Jesus give himself credibility in his speech? What does he declare to the Jews?
3. Spend time today thinking about whether you judge by appearances or see what's really important.

Day 4: John 7:25-30

1. What word or phrase stands out to you from this passage? Why?
2. Why are the Pharisees so upset? Why can't they seize Jesus and stop him from teaching?
3. Spend time today thinking about God's power and how he is in control of everything.

Day 5: John 7:31-36

1. What word or phrase stands out to you from this passage? Why?
2. What does Jesus allude to in this passage? Do the Jews understand him?
3. Spend time today thinking about how well you understand God's Word.

Day 6: John 7:37-43

1. What word or phrase stands out to you from this passage? Why?
2. Why do you think Jesus said what he did on the last day (of the Feast)? Don't you think people were satisfied after seven days of eating and drinking?
3. Spend time today thinking about the times you've sought satisfaction in food or drink and ended up empty.

Day 7: John 7:1-43

Read through the whole passage and write out the verse that spoke to you the most this week. Meditate on that verse today—and for an extra challenge, memorize it!

From *Studies on the Go* by Laurie Polich. Permission granted to reproduce this page for use in buyer's youth group only. Copyright 2006, Youth Specialties.

12. FINGER POINTING

John 8:1-11

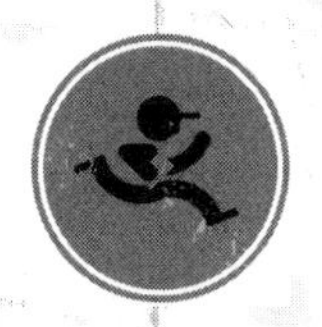

Overview: Imagine the scene. People are sitting in the temple listening to Jesus. Suddenly the Pharisees storm in, dragging a scantily clothed woman to the front of the group. They give the announcement of the law: "Moses commanded us to stone such women." They look at Jesus. "What do you say?"

Suddenly Jesus bends down and begins to write. Finally he gets up and replies, "If any one of you is without sin, let him be the first to throw a stone." Then he bends down again.

The focus has shifted from the woman. Everyone is focused on himself. One by one the people walk away, and the woman is left alone. No one is left to condemn her—except for Jesus. Instead Jesus speaks words that are filled with grace. "Neither do I condemn you," he says. "Go now and leave your life of sin."

In this session your students will learn that these words aren't just for the woman. They are for them, too.

SHARE

Warm-Up Qs

1. What was your most embarrassing moment? Do you remember how it felt?
2. Have you ever felt judged by someone? Without naming names, share your experience with the group.
3. Have you ever been in a situation where your friends were ganging up on someone (e.g., being mean to that person, avoiding him or her, or gossiping about him or her)? If so, did you join in? How did you feel afterward?

OBSERVE

Observation Qs

4. Read John 8:1-6. What is Jesus doing when the Pharisees bring the woman in? Where do they make her stand?
5. What do the Pharisees ask Jesus? (vv. 4-5) According to v. 6, why do they ask him this question? Does Jesus answer their question? What does he do?
6. Read vv. 7-11. What does Jesus say to the Pharisees and teachers of the law? What does he do next? How do the Pharisees respond? Who responds first?
7. Who is left after Jesus' challenge? What three things does he say to the woman?

THINK

Interpretation Qs

8. What do you think motivated the Pharisees and teachers of the law to bring this woman to Jesus? Do you think they were really concerned about her actions? Why or why not?
9. What is the "trap" the Pharisees try to set for Jesus? (Look closely at what they ask him in vv. 4-5.) What do they hope Jesus will do?

10. Why do you think Jesus bent down and started writing before he responded to the Pharisees? What do you think the crowd was doing at that moment?
11. Based on what happened in this passage, do you think Jesus cared about the woman's sin? Why or why not? As you evaluate his words and actions, what do you think he was most concerned about?

APPLY

Application Qs

12. Who do you most relate with in this passage—the Pharisees, the woman, or the crowd? Who do you least relate with? Why?
13. Do you struggle more with judging others or feeling judged? Why?
14. Would you be comfortable if your church friends saw everything you did in your relationships with the opposite sex? Why or why not?
15. How do Jesus' words in v. 11 hit home with you? Which do you need to hear more: "Neither do I condemn you" or "Go now and leave your life of sin"? Why?

DO

Optional Activity: Try a creative closing idea. Get a bunch of smooth stones (big enough to write on, but not too big) and markers for your group. Pass them out and have your students write a sin with which they struggle on their stone (either a word, initials, or a picture—something only they know). Then have your students stand up and squeeze their stones tightly in their hands. While the students continue squeezing, explain that you're going to give a quick benediction, and then they should leave the meeting in silence, each of them releasing their tight grips and dropping their stones into a large bag by the door that you will immediately dispose of without looking inside. Your benediction is, "Go and sin no more."

Day 1: John 8:1-4

1. What word or phrase stands out to you from this passage? Why?
2. Why do the Pharisees bring the woman in front of the crowd? Where is the man?
3. Spend time today thinking about a time when you did something wrong with someone else, and only one of you got caught. How did it feel?

Day 2: John 8:5-6

1. What word or phrase stands out to you from these verses? Why?
2. Why do you think Jesus bent down and started writing? Do you think he had a purpose in doing this?
3. Spend time today thinking about the ways God has come alongside you and supported you when you were going through difficult times.

Day 3: John 8:7-9

1. What word or phrase stands out to you from this passage? Why?
2. How does Jesus change the focus of what's happening in this passage? Why do the older people leave first?
3. Spend time today thinking about whether you tend to be more critical of others or yourself.

Day 4: John 8:10-11

1. What word or phrase stands out to you from these verses? Why?
2. How do you think the woman felt about Jesus after this experience? How would you have felt?
3. Spend time today thinking about Jesus' forgiveness and his desire for you to "leave your life of sin."

Day 5: John 8:12-21

1. What word or phrase stands out to you from this passage? Why?
2. How do Jesus' words about judgment (vv. 15-16) relate to what happened in the previous encounter with the woman?
3. Spend time today thinking about how God's judgment is different from the way people judge us.

Day 6: John 8:22-30

1. What word or phrase stands out to you from this passage? Why?
2. What are the different responses to Jesus' words in this passage?
3. Spend time today thinking about how you would have responded to Jesus in this passage, and what it was that caused you to put your faith in him. (See v. 30.)

Day 7: John 8:1-30

Read through the whole passage and write out the verse that spoke to you the most this week. Meditate on that verse today—and for an extra challenge, memorize it!

From *Studies on the Go* by Laurie Polich. Permission granted to reproduce this page for use in buyer's youth group only. Copyright 2006, Youth Specialties.

13. FREEDOM AND SLAVERY

John 8:31-59

Overview: Sin never delivers the freedom it promises. Instead it makes you its slave. But that's not what students think about when they're headed down sin's path. And that's why this session is so important.

Jesus says, "Everyone who sins is a slave to sin." (v. 34) If we keep giving in to the same sin, eventually we'll experience the consequences. And usually they're consequences we don't choose.

I heard an alcoholic share what happened when he finally experienced the consequences of his drinking. The time came when he no longer wanted the alcohol; he needed it. He described it by saying, "There was a knock on the door, and I opened it to find a bunch of bottles of liquor with a note. The note read, 'We've been happy to serve you for a while. But from now on, you'll serve us.'"

That's a perfect illustration of what Jesus talks about in this passage. He also talks about how to break free. He says, "If the Son sets you free, you will be free indeed." (v. 36) The only condition to this promise is that we must claim it.

SHARE

Warm-Up Qs

1. Bob Dylan wrote a song called "Gotta Serve Somebody," and his lyrics note that everyone serves something or someone. Do you think that's true? Why or why not?
2. What is your definition of freedom? What is your definition of slavery?
3. Do you consider yourself a free person or not? Why?

OBSERVE

Observation Qs

4. Read John 8:31-41. What does Jesus say sets us free? (v. 32) How do the Jews respond? (v. 33) How does Jesus define slavery and freedom in vv. 34-36?
5. Read vv. 42-47. What is Jesus responding to in this speech? (v. 41) What judgment does he place on the Jews who are skeptical of him? (vv. 44-47) What is Jesus' reasoning for saying they don't belong to God? (vv. 42-43, 46-47)
6. Read vv. 48-58. What accusation do the Jews place on Jesus? (v. 48) What is their argument for saying this? (vv. 52-53) How do they use Abraham in their argument?
7. What does Jesus say about Abraham in v. 56? How do the Jews respond? What does Jesus say that causes them to get mad enough to pick up stones to stone him? (v. 58)

THINK

Interpretation Qs

8. Why are the Jews so mad at Jesus in this passage? Do you feel they were unreasonable, or do you understand why they got so upset?
9. Look at vv. 31-32. Why does Jesus say obedience to him equals freedom? Do you think of obedience to someone as freedom? Why or why not?

10. Look at Jesus' words in v. 51. Why do you think this statement drew such an extreme reaction from the Pharisees? (v. 52) Do you think they were feeling threatened by Jesus, or did they just think he was crazy?
11. When Jesus says, "Before Abraham was, I AM," (v. 58) what do you think he was saying? Do you think he used the present tense on purpose? If so, why? (Also see Exodus 3:14.)

APPLY

Application Qs

12. Based on what Jesus says in this passage, do you think it's possible to just think of him as a good religious teacher? Why or why not?
13. If you were a Pharisee in this passage, would you have been more or less convinced that Jesus is who he said he is? Why?
14. Would you say you're living the kind of life Jesus describes in vv. 31-32? If so, are you experiencing freedom? If not, what is keeping you from it?

DO

Optional Activity: Invite a Christian who is an ex-addict (in recovery) to come share his or her story with your group. Have the person share when he or she became a slave to the addiction, and what it was that caused him or her to break free. Have the visitor also share how faith contributes to his or her recovery.

Day 1: John 8:31-35

1. What word or phrase stands out to you from this passage? Why?
2. What do you think it means to be a "slave to sin"?
3. Spend time today thinking about whether or not you are a slave to any sin in your life.

Day 2: John 8:36-41

1. What word or phrase stands out to you from this passage? Why?
2. What are the Jews in this passage leaning on for their status with God? What does Jesus say to them?
3. Spend time today thinking about what you're leaning on in your relationship with God—is it your good works? Being in a Christian family? Or your own relationship with Christ?

Day 3: John 8:42-47

1. What word or phrase stands out to you from this passage? Why?
2. According to Jesus in this passage, who is able to hear him clearly? Do you feel you are able to hear and understand his words?
3. Spend time today thinking about the way you read the Bible and Jesus' words, and whether or not you hear them as the words of God.

Day 4: John 8:48-51

1. What word or phrase stands out to you from this passage? Why?
2. What does Jesus argue in this passage? What is his defense?
3. Spend time today thinking about Jesus' relationship to God, and how they glorify each other.

Day 5: John 8:52-55

1. What word or phrase stands out to you from this passage? Why?
2. Why do the Jews in this passage think Jesus is demon possessed? What are their reasons?
3. Spend time today thinking about what you would have thought of Jesus if you were on earth when he was. Would you have thought he was crazy, or that he was the Son of God?

Day 6: John 8:56-59

1. What word or phrase stands out to you from this passage? Why?
2. What does Jesus say that really makes the Jews mad in this passage? Why do you think it made them so mad?
3. Spend time today thinking about the eternal nature of Jesus—how he was here before you were born, so he is here, with you, right now.

Day 7: John 8:31-59

Read through the whole passage and write out the verse that spoke to you the most this week. Meditate on that verse today—and for an extra challenge, memorize it!

From *Studies on the Go* by Laurie Polich. Permission granted to reproduce this page for use in buyer's youth group only. Copyright 2006, Youth Specialties.

14. EYES TO SEE

John 9:1-41

Overview: In John 9:39 Jesus says, "For judgment I have come into this world, so that the blind will see and those who see will become blind." That's exactly what happens in this passage.

At the beginning of the chapter, the blind man is not only physically blind; he is spiritually blind, too. He has no idea who Jesus is. Jesus heals him physically, but he also gives him eyes to see spiritually. The man reveals his newfound faith in Christ when he says to the Pharisees, "Do you want to become his disciples, too?" (v. 27) His question indicates that he has become a disciple, and he challenges the Pharisees to join him.

As the blind man's vision gets clearer and clearer, the Pharisees' vision gets foggier and foggier because they refuse to accept his testimony. In the end the blind man ends up with more spiritual vision than the Pharisees.

From this session your students will learn that having spiritual vision is more important than having physical vision. And having narrow vision can end up costing you your sight.

SHARE
Warm-Up Qs

1. If you had to be deaf, mute, or blind, which would you choose? Which would you least like to be?
2. Do you feel that people's physical conditions are tied to their spiritual conditions? If so, how?
3. Do you think it's worse to be physically blind or spiritually blind? Why?

OBSERVE
Observation Qs

4. Read John 9:1-12. Look at the question the disciples ask in v. 2. What is their assumption? How does Jesus respond? (v. 3)
5. How is the blind man healed? (vv. 6-7) How do his neighbors respond to his healing? (vv. 8-9)
6. Read vv. 13-34. How many times do the Pharisees ask the man about his healing? (vv. 15, 17, 26). Who else do they ask? (v. 18) What response do they keep getting? How do they react? (vv. 28, 34)
7. Read vv. 35-41. How does Jesus reveal himself to the man? (vv. 35-37) What does he say about physical and spiritual blindness? (v. 39)

THINK
Interpretation Qs

8. Look at what Jesus says in v. 3. Do you think his statement means that every physical ailment is for God's work to be displayed? Why or why not?
9. How are the responses to the man's healing (vv. 8-9) similar to the responses to God's miracles today?
10. As you observe the Pharisees in this chapter, do you think they were looking for evidence to believe in Jesus? Why or why not? (Look especially at vv. 15-34.)

11. Look at v. 39. What do you think Jesus means by this statement? (Look also at vv. 40-41.)

APPLY

Application Qs

12. Would you describe yourself as being spiritually blind or having spiritual eyesight? Why?
13. How does this chapter affect the way you think about God's healing? Does everyone who asks for healing receive it? What do you think is the purpose of the man's healing?
14. Do you think God cares more about your physical self or your spiritual self? As you look at the way you live, which do you care about most?
15. How do you feel about the statement Jesus makes in v. 39? Does it bother you to think of Jesus coming into the world for judgment? Why or why not?

DO

Optional Activity: At the end of the study, pass out blindfolds and have everyone put them on for 15 minutes. (You can do this before the application questions if you want the activity to be longer.) Serve snacks and let the students mingle. Then have them take their blindfolds off and share what it felt like to be blind and then to see. (Here are some questions to get the ball rolling: What did they notice? What frustrated them? What did they see first when the exercise was over?)

Day 1: John 9:1-5

1. What word or phrase stands out to you from this passage? Why?
2. What was the reason this man was blind? What does that tell you about the reason for our physical ailments?
3. Spend time today thinking about how our weaknesses and disabilities can point to God's work in our lives.

Day 2: John 9:6-12

1. What word or phrase stands out to you from this passage? Why?
2. How do others react to the man who was healed? How is it similar to the way people often respond today?
3. Spend time today thinking about whether you give God credit for healing (and other miracles), or if you think things like this "just happen."

Day 3: John 9:13-16

1. What word or phrase stands out to you from this passage? Why?
2. Why do the Pharisees refuse to accept that Jesus healed the man?
3. Spend time today thinking about the ways we "put God in a box" and don't accept him when he works differently than we think he should.

Day 4: John 9:17-23

1. What word or phrase stands out to you from this passage? Why?
2. Why are the man's parents brought into the investigation? How do they show their intimidation of the Pharisees?
3. Spend time today thinking about the ways you have been intimidated in sharing your beliefs.

Day 5: John 9:24-34

1. What word or phrase stands out to you from this passage? Why?
2. How does the man show boldness in his witness for Christ? Do you think you would have responded this way?
3. Spend time today thinking about how you can be a bolder witness for Christ's work in your life.

Day 6: John 9:35-41

1. What word or phrase stands out to you from this passage? Why?
2. How do the blind see—and those who see become blind—in this passage?
3. Spend time today thinking about your spiritual vision and whether or not you see things from an earthly or heavenly perspective.

Day 7: John 9:1-41

Read through the whole passage and write out the verse that spoke to you the most this week. Meditate on that verse today—and for an extra challenge, memorize it!

From *Studies on the Go* by Laurie Polich. Permission granted to reproduce this page for use in buyer's youth group only. Copyright 2006, Youth Specialties.

15. THE GOOD SHEPHERD

John 10:1-33

Overview: Sheep are not the brightest of creatures. And because of that, they need a little help. Usually that help comes in the form of a shepherd. That's the image Jesus borrows in this passage. The good news is that he's our shepherd. The bad news is that we're like sheep.

Sometimes a shepherd guides sheep gently, using his staff to direct their path. Other times he has to use a firmer touch. But when sheep go too far in the wrong direction, the shepherd goes to great lengths to get them back.

Jesus calls himself our shepherd to let us know how much he cares for us. He also "shepherds" us to provide the direction we need. In this session your students will determine where they stand in relation to the shepherd. They'll also decide what position they have in his flock. Even if they feel far away, they'll discover in this passage that their distance doesn't temper his love. And he'll always be committed to getting them back.

SHARE

Warm-Up Qs

1. When you're with your friends, do you tend to be a leader or a follower? Why?
2. Is there anyone in your life whom you have followed (a friend, a teacher, an athlete, a musician, etc.)? What was it about that person that made you follow him or her?
3. What are three words you would use to describe sheep? Why those words?

OBSERVE

Observation Qs

4. Read John 10:1-10. What does Jesus say about sheep in this passage? (vv. 3-5) What metaphor does he use to describe himself? (v. 7)
5. Read vv. 11-21. What other metaphor does Jesus use to describe himself? (vv. 11, 14) What does he say he will do for his sheep? (v. 11) How many times does he repeat this in this passage?
6. How do the Jews react to Jesus' illustration? (vv. 19-21)
7. Read vv. 22-30. What does Jesus say about "his sheep"? (v. 27) What will Jesus give his sheep? (v. 28) Why does Jesus say none of his sheep will get snatched? (v. 29)

THINK

Interpretation Qs

8. Why does Jesus say he is the gate for the sheep (v. 7) and shepherd of the sheep? (v. 11) Can he be both of these things? If so, how?
9. In vv. 11-13, Jesus contrasts the good shepherd with the hired hand. Who do you think the "hired hand" symbolizes? Why do you think Jesus gives this illustration?

10. Look at what Jesus says in v. 16. Who do you think the "other sheep" are?
11. Look at what the Jews ask in v. 24, and what Jesus says in v. 30. Do you think Jesus answered their question? Why do they want to stone him? (vv. 31-33) Do you think they really wanted to know the truth? Why or why not?

APPLY

Application Qs

12. If you were a sheep in Jesus' flock, where would you be?
    - A. Right behind him (following him closely)
    - B. In the back (following him from afar)
    - C. Outside the pen (not following him at all)
13. Do you think of Jesus as your shepherd? Why or why not? In what ways has he led you?
14. In this passage Jesus says his sheep know and recognize his voice. Would you say that's true in your own life? If so, how does Jesus communicate with you?
15. If someone said to you, "Jesus was just a great religious teacher," what would you say? (See v. 30.) What do you think our choices are in what we think about Jesus?

DO

Optional Activity: Voice recognition game: For fun, play some famous voices for your students (you can do this from your computer, DVD player, CD player, or iPod). See how many they can recognize. Then have students list five people in their lives whose voices they would recognize right away, and share what it is that makes a voice recognizable to them. Finally, ask them what they think would help them recognize God's voice.

Day 1: John 10:1-6

1. What word or phrase stands out to you from this passage? Why?
2. Can you identify the shepherd and the sheep in this passage? If so, who are they?
3. Spend time today thinking about how Jesus shepherds you—and the ways you hear his voice.

Day 2: John 10:7-10

1. What word or phrase stands out to you from this passage? Why?
2. How does Jesus mix metaphors in this passage? Is this metaphor compatible with the previous passage? If so, how?
3. Spend time today thinking about Jesus as the gate—and what that means for the people in your life who don't have a relationship with God.

Day 3: John 10:11-13

1. What word or phrase stands out to you from this passage? Why?
2. What's the difference between the shepherd and the hired hand? Who do you think the "hired hand" is?
3. Spend time today thinking about who would be a "hired hand" in your life, and how God cares for you in a deeper, greater way.

Day 4: John 10:14-21

1. What word or phrase stands out to you from this passage? Why?
2. Who do you think the sheep are that are "not of this sheep pen"? How does Jesus show his love for all people in this passage?
3. Spend time today thinking about the people in different cultures and different denominations that Jesus considers "his sheep." What is the determining factor that makes someone "a sheep"?

Day 5: John 9:22-33

1. What word or phrase stands out to you from this passage? Why?
2. When the Jews ask Jesus to tell them if he's the Christ, do you think they really wanted to know? Why or why not?
3. Spend time today thinking about how people want God to come to them on their terms (so they can control him). Do you?

Day 6: John 9:34-42

1. What word or phrase stands out to you from this passage? Why?
2. How does Jesus reveal himself as God's Son in this passage? How do the Jews react?
3. Spend time today thinking about whether or not you have a hard time accepting Jesus' authority as your God. Are his words welcome in your life?

Day 7: John 9:1-42

Read through the whole passage and write out the verse that spoke to you the most this week. Meditate on that verse today—and for an extra challenge, memorize it!

From *Studies on the Go* by Laurie Polich. Permission granted to reproduce this page for use in buyer's youth group only. Copyright 2006, Youth Specialties.

16. FROM DEATH TO LIFE

John 11:1-44

Overview: At first glance Jesus does something in this passage that doesn't seem to make sense. Mary and Martha have made a special effort to get word to him that Lazarus is sick. Yet verse 6 reads, "When he heard that Lazarus was sick, he stayed where he was two more days."

When Jesus finally arrives in Bethany, Lazarus is no longer sick—he's dead. Martha comes to meet Jesus, and you can almost hear her disappointment when she says, "Lord, if you had been here, my brother would not have died." What Martha couldn't have seen was that Lazarus' death was exactly what Jesus was waiting for to do his miracle. Mary and Martha wanted their brother healed; Jesus wanted more. Sometimes that's the way it is with us.

In this session your students will see that our plans for God pale in comparison to God's plans for us. And because of that, we have to trust. Sometimes our plans have to die so God's plans can begin. That's when true miracles happen.

SHARE

Warm-Up Qs

1. Have you ever been disappointed that God didn't show up when you wanted him to? If so, when?
2. What's the most amazing thing you've ever seen God do? What (if anything) do you wish you could see God do?
3. When tragedy strikes, do you tend to be more logical or emotional? Do you feel first and then think or think first and then feel?

OBSERVE

Observation Qs

4. Read John 11:1-16. What does Jesus do when he hears the news about Lazarus? (v. 6) What does he say to the disciples about Lazarus' condition? (v. 11) Do they understand what he's saying? (v. 13)
5. Read vv. 17-37. What does Martha do when she hears Jesus is coming? (v. 20) How does she show her faith in spite of her disappointment? (vv. 22, 27) When Jesus says what will happen to Lazarus, what does Martha think will happen? (vv. 23-24)
6. What does Mary do when she hears Jesus has arrived? (vv. 31-32) How does Jesus respond? (vv. 33-35)
7. Read vv. 38-44. How does Martha react when Jesus has the stone removed? (v. 39) What does he say to her? (v. 40) What does he do next?

THINK

Interpretation Qs

8. How do you think Mary and Martha felt when they found out Jesus stayed two days after hearing the news about Lazarus?

9. How does Mary respond to this situation differently from Martha? Do you think Jesus thought one was better than the other? How do their responses affect him?
10. Why do you think Jesus cried with Mary and Martha when he knew what he was about to do? (vv. 33-35) What does this reveal about Jesus?
11. Do you think this miracle was more for Lazarus' sake or for everyone else's? Why do you think Jesus raised him from the dead?

APPLY

Application Qs

12. To whom do you relate most in this passage—Mary or Martha? Why?
13. Do you ever feel like God isn't answering your prayer because he doesn't care? What insights (if any) does this passage give you about that?
14. When God holds back from answering our prayers the way we want, do you think there's always a reason? Why or why not? What might be some of those reasons?
15. Based on what you learned from this passage, what do you think is the purpose of God's miracles on earth? Do you understand them differently now? Why or why not?

DO

Optional Activity: If possible, take your group to a cemetery and read this passage together one more time. Have your students imagine what it would be like if the ground broke open and a dead body became alive again. What would they do? What emotions would they feel? Who would they tell first? Who would believe them? Who wouldn't believe them?

Day 1: John 11:1-6

1. What word or phrase stands out to you from this passage? Why?
2. How do you think Mary and Martha felt when they realized Jesus got their message and didn't leave for two more days?
3. Spend time today thinking about the times it appears God doesn't care when, in fact, there's a reason he's doing what he's doing.

Day 2: John 11:7-16

1. What word or phrase stands out to you from this passage? Why?
2. What misunderstandings do you see between the disciples and Jesus in this passage? Why don't they understand him?
3. Spend time today thinking about how people can misunderstand Jesus' teachings. Have you ever misunderstood something you read in the Bible?

Day 3: John 11:17-22

1. What word or phrase stands out to you from this passage? Why?
2. How does Martha show her faith in this passage?
3. Spend time today thinking about the ways you can show your faith to God.

Day 4: John 11:23-27

1. What word or phrase stands out to you from this passage? Why?
2. How does Jesus describe himself in this passage? How do you think Martha felt when she heard him say this?
3. Spend time today thinking about Jesus' power extending beyond death, and whether or not it changes the way you feel about your death.

Day 5: John 11:28-37

1. What word or phrase stands out to you from this passage? Why?
2. Why does Jesus weep in this passage if he already knows what he's going to do? What does that tell you about him?
3. Spend time today thinking about God's compassion for you when you're sad.

Day 6: John 11:38-44

1. What word or phrase stands out to you from this passage? Why?
2. How do you think people reacted when Lazarus came out of the tomb? How would you have reacted?
3. Spend time today thinking about whether you live as though God is capable of doing miracles.

Day 7: John 11:1-44

Read through the whole passage and write out the verse that spoke to you the most this week. Meditate on that verse today—and for an extra challenge, memorize it!

From *Studies on the Go* by Laurie Polich. Permission granted to reproduce this page for use in buyer's youth group only. Copyright 2006, Youth Specialties.

17. A DIFFERENT KING

John 12:1-19

Overview: In this passage Judas chastises Mary for honoring Jesus in an extravagant way. She takes expensive perfume, worth about $12,000 by today's standards, and pours it on Jesus' feet. It was an act of worship that people may have seen as wasteful and unnecessary. Judas says what others were thinking when he asks, "Why wasn't the perfume sold and the money given to the poor?" Yet Jesus, friend of the poor, dismisses Judas' words and commends Mary's act of worship. Why?

Jesus realizes people have needs that are more than physical; we are emotional and spiritual beings, too. Jesus accepts Mary's anointing as an act of symbolism and sacrifice, and he honors her for it. Her act illustrates our need and God's desire for creative expressions of worship. But perfume was not only associated with festivity; it was used in burials, too. This is a sign that Jesus was going to be a very different king.

As your students read on, they will realize this anointing was preparation for his death. And his way to the throne would be the cross.

SHARE

Warm-Up Qs

1. What words come to your mind when you think of the word *king*?
2. If you were in charge of planning a parade for a king or president, how would you have him or her transported? Why?
3. Have you ever spent money on something that other people thought was a waste? If so, what was it? Why did you spend your money on it?

OBSERVE

Observation Qs

4. Read John 12:1-11. Who is the guest of honor at the dinner given in Bethany? (v. 2) Who is there? Who is serving?
5. What does Mary do at this dinner? (v. 3) What does Judas say after she's done? (vv. 4-5) How does Jesus respond? (vv. 7-8)
6. Read vv. 12-19. How does Jesus arrive in Jerusalem? (v. 14) What prophecy does this fulfill? (v. 15) When do the disciples realize the prophecy has been fulfilled? (v. 16)
7. What does the crowd do when Jesus arrives? (vv. 12-13) What story do they spread to others? (v. 17) How do the Pharisees react to all this? (v. 19)

THINK

Interpretation Qs

8. What do you think the mood was at the dinner given by Mary, Martha, and Lazarus? Why do you think they wanted to honor Jesus? (vv. 1-2)
9. Look at what Jesus says about Mary's actions in vv. 7-8. What do you think he means? Do you think people knew what he was saying? Why or why not?

10. Why does Jesus arrive this way in his moment of glory? (v. 14) Do you think God had a reason for this? (v. 15) Why didn't he choose a greater way for him to arrive?
11. Do you think the story about Lazarus had a greater effect on people than the other miracles? Why or why not? Why was it such a threat to the Pharisees? (vv. 9-10)

APPLY

Application Qs

12. How would you have felt if you saw Mary do what she did to Jesus? Do you think you would have questioned her actions? Why or why not?
13. Have you ever seen someone do something in worship that seemed too extravagant or made you uncomfortable? If so, how does Mary's worship compare with what you saw?
14. There is an argument that Christians should stop spending money on churches and spend it on feeding the poor. Do you agree with this? Do you think Jesus agrees with this?
15. Do you think if Jesus had been a less humble, more public king, he would have drawn more followers? Why or why not?

DO

Optional Activity: Either before this study or before next week's study, tell your students to choose one thing to bring to the group to honor Jesus. (It could be a symbol, an object, a song, a poem... they can be as creative as they want.) When you gather, have all students talk about what they brought, and why they brought it to honor Jesus. End with a time of prayer.

Day 1: John 12:1-2

1. What word or phrase stands out to you from these verses? Why?
2. What formerly dead person is present at this dinner? How do you think people were responding to him?
3. Spend time today thinking about what it would be like to come back from the dead. Would you want to? Why or why not?

Day 2: John 12:3-6

1. What word or phrase stands out to you from this passage? Why?
2. Who objects to what Mary did in this passage? How do you think you would have felt if you were there?
3. Spend time today thinking about when it is appropriate to be extravagant in our worship. What does that mean to you?

Day 3: John 12:7-8

1. What word or phrase stands out to you from these verses? Why?
2. Do Jesus' words about the poor in this passage surprise you? Why or why not?
3. Spend time today thinking about how loving God leads us to care about people around us. Who do you know that needs you today?

Day 4: John 12:9-13

1. What word or phrase stands out to you from this passage? Why?
2. What contrast do you see in the way people respond to Jesus in these verses?
3. Spend time today thinking about how people respond differently to Jesus. What responses have you seen?

Day 5: John 12:14-16

1. What word or phrase stands out to you from this passage? Why?
2. Does it surprise you that Jesus would ride on a donkey? Why or why not?
3. Spend time today thinking about the ways Jesus showed his humility while he was on earth.

Day 6: John 12:17-19

1. What word or phrase stands out to you from this passage? Why?
2. How do the Pharisees indicate in this passage that they feel threatened by Jesus?
3. Spend time today thinking about the way people feel "threatened" by Jesus today. What makes them feel this way?

Day 7: John 12:1-19

Read through the whole passage and write out the verse that spoke to you the most this week. Meditate on that verse today—and for an extra challenge, memorize it!

From *Studies on the Go* by Laurie Polich. Permission granted to reproduce this page for use in buyer's youth group only. Copyright 2006, Youth Specialties.

18. TIME TO DECIDE

John 12:20-50

Overview: In this passage Jesus gives the crowd one last chance to consider his claims. He expresses the urgency of the moment when he says, "You are going to have the light just a little longer. Walk while you have the light, before darkness overtakes you." (v. 35) His words challenge the Jews to make their choice.

This same decision faces your students today. And in a way it's just as urgent. We don't know when our lives will end, but at that time there will be no more opportunities to make a decision. Our decision will have already been made.

This session shows that while we are here, the light is available to us if we want it. All we have to do is believe in Jesus. He says that when people believe in him, they believe in the One who sent him (v. 44). But we must respond in faith for the relationship to begin. Only those who choose not to believe will end up in darkness. But that's not God's choice for us. How we respond to Jesus will determine our fate. And this is a choice we all make for ourselves.

SHARE

Warm-Up Qs

1. What is the hardest decision you've ever had to make? What made it so hard?
2. If you were in a car with God, would you want to be in the driver's seat—or would you want him to be in the driver's seat? Why?
3. What do you think it means to walk in the light versus walking in the dark? What does it mean for you?

OBSERVE

Observation Qs

4. Read John 12:20-33. What hour has come according to Jesus in v. 23? What illustration does he give after he says this? (v. 24) What does v. 27 say about Jesus' emotions at this time? What does v. 27 say about his resolve (or decision)?
5. What happens in v. 28? What does the crowd hear? (v. 29) What does Jesus say? (v. 30)
6. Read vv. 34-50. What four things does Jesus say about light in this passage? (vv. 35-36, 46) What does Jesus say people need to do to not be in darkness?
7. What response does Jesus get from people? (vv. 37, 42) What do vv. 38-40 say about the people who didn't believe? What do vv. 42-43 say about the people who did believe?

THINK

Interpretation Qs

8. Look at v. 24. Do you think Jesus is speaking about himself in this verse? If so, how? What do you think he's saying?
9. In v. 25, Jesus says a man must hate his life in order to keep it for eternal life. What do you think he means by this?
10. What is the light Jesus is talking about in vv. 35-36? What do you think Jesus means when he says the people will only have

the light a little while longer? (v. 35) What happens to people who put their trust in the light? (v. 36) What does trusting the light mean?

11. Look at vv. 37-40. Do you think people had a choice in believing or not believing? Or was the choice made for them? How do you interpret these verses?

APPLY

Application Qs

12. How do you interpret Jesus' words in v. 25 for yourself? Can it be bad to "love your life"? How do you think he wants you to feel about your life?
13. As you look at vv. 37-40, do you think our decision to come to faith is controlled by God—or us? Does this mean we should still share our faith with others? Why or why not?
14. Look at what vv. 42-43 say about those who believed. Are you ever embarrassed to talk about your faith because of what others might think? Is v. 43 true for you—or not?
15. As you look at Jesus' words in vv. 47-48, how does our relationship with Jesus impact the way God judges us? What about our actions? Which is more important?

DO

Optional Activity: Ask your students how they would respond if God asked them how he should judge them. What are the reasons they should be judged favorably? What are the reasons they shouldn't be judged favorably? (Give them time to think and write down their reflections if they want.)

Day 1: John 12:20-26

1. What word or phrase stands out to you from this passage? Why?
2. How does Jesus say he will be glorified? What analogy does he give?
3. Spend time today thinking about what happens to a seed when it's planted in the ground. How is it an analogy for our lives as Christians?

Day 2: John 12:27-33

1. What word or phrase stands out to you from this passage? Why?
2. What does Jesus say was the reason he came to earth?
3. Spend time today thinking about Jesus' willingness to come to earth to die for you.

Day 3: John 12:34-36

1. What word or phrase stands out to you from this passage? Why?
2. What do you think it means to "walk in the light"? Would you say you do this?
3. Spend time today thinking about how you can spend more time walking in the light and less time walking in the dark.

Day 4: John 12:37-41

1. What word or phrase stands out to you from this passage? Why?
2. How did the Jews who rejected Jesus fulfill Old Testament prophecy?
3. Spend time today thinking about whether your eyes have ever been blinded—or your heart hardened—to evidence of God's work. How can you keep yourself open?

Day 5: John 12:42-46

1. What word or phrase stands out to you from this passage? Why?
2. Why were people afraid to confess their faith in Jesus?
3. Spend time today thinking about the times you're afraid to confess your faith in Jesus. How can you be bolder?

Day 6: John 12:47-50

1. What word or phrase stands out to you from this passage? Why?
2. What was Jesus' purpose in coming to earth?
3. Spend time today thinking about who needs to hear about God's love rather than his judgment. Is there anyone with whom you can share this good news?

Day 7: John 12:20-50

Read through the whole passage and write out the verse that spoke to you the most this week. Meditate on that verse today—and for an extra challenge, memorize it!

From *Studies on the Go* by Laurie Polich. Permission granted to reproduce this page for use in buyer's youth group only. Copyright 2006, Youth Specialties.

19. THE WAY TO GREATNESS

John 13:1-17

Overview: Jesus knows he's about to go to the Father. He's with his disciples for the very last time. Now he wants to show them his power in a way they'll never forget. He does it by washing their feet.

Verse 3 says, "Jesus knew that the Father had put all things under his power." You'd think the next verse would say, "So he told his disciples to worship him." But Jesus wants his disciples to see a different kind of power. It foreshadows what they're going to see on the cross.

Jesus wraps a towel around his waist and bends down to wash the grime off their feet. You can almost hear the horror in Peter's voice when he says, "Lord, are you going to wash my feet?" Jesus tells Peter that unless he washes his feet, Peter has no part in him. The disciples learn that footwashing is part of discipleship.

Today there are many ways to "wash people's feet." Your students will learn that in this session. Jesus says, "I have set you an example that you should do as I have done for you." We are left to translate his words into action.

SHARE

Warm-Up Qs

1. If someone you admired offered to wash your hands or your feet, which would you have them do? Why?
2. What are three qualities that make a great leader? What are the qualities that make someone a bad leader?
3. If you had to pick the greatest leader throughout history, who would you choose? Why?

OBSERVE

Observation Qs

4. Read John 13:1-5. According to v. 1, what is about to happen to Jesus? What is he going to show his disciples?
5. Look at vv. 3-5. Where do you see a contrast of power in these verses?
6. Read vv. 6-11. What does Peter initially say to Jesus about washing his feet? What causes Peter to change his mind? (v. 8)
7. Read vv. 12-17. What example does Jesus set in this passage? What does he tell the disciples to do?

THINK

Interpretation Qs

8. Why do you think Jesus washed the disciples' feet first and then explained it? Why didn't he explain it first—and then do it?
9. Look at Jesus' first response to Peter in v. 7. What do you think he means by this?
10. If Jesus already knew what Judas was going to do, why do you think he washed his feet? (vv. 2, 10) What insight does this give you about Jesus' love?
11. What do you think Jesus means when he tells his disciples to wash each other's feet? (v. 14) Is he being literal? Why or why not?

APPLY

Application Qs

12. If you had been one of the disciples in this passage, do you think you would have spoken up (like Peter) or been silent (like the rest)? Why?
13. What would be an example of "washing someone's feet"? How do we do this today?
14. If Jesus was going to do something like this in our culture, what do you think he would do?
15. Look at Jesus' promise in v. 17. Have you ever been blessed by serving others? If so, when?

DO

Optional Activity: Plan a footwashing for your group. Get a basin and a few towels, and have everyone sit in a circle. One by one, have each person get his or her own feet washed, and experience washing someone else's feet. Debrief by asking them how they felt during the experience, and which felt more awkward—getting their feet washed or washing someone else's feet. Which did they prefer? Why? (You may want to warn your group a week in advance that you will be doing this.)

Day 1: John 13:1

1. What word or phrase stands out to you from this verse? Why?
2. What does Jesus want to show his disciples before he leaves?
3. Spend time today thinking about what you would want to do if you knew you were leaving this world.

Day 2: John 13:2-4

1. What word or phrase stands out to you from this passage? Why?
2. What contrast in power do you see in these verses?
3. Spend time today thinking about the ways God shows us his power and how different it is from the way the world defines power.

Day 3: John 13:5-9

1. What word or phrase stands out to you from this passage? Why?
2. Why doesn't Peter want Jesus to wash his feet? What changes his mind?
3. Spend time today thinking about how Jesus set an example for us when he washed his disciples' feet. What would this mean in today's culture?

Day 4: John 13:10-11

1. What word or phrase stands out to you from these verses? Why?
2. How does Jesus refer to Judas in this passage? What does he say about him?
3. Spend time today thinking about what it means to be "clean" the way Jesus speaks of in this passage. Are you?

Day 5: John 13:12-14

1. What word or phrase stands out to you from this passage? Why?
2. What do you think Jesus means when he tells the disciples to wash one another's feet?
3. Spend time today thinking about the ways we can wash other people's feet. How can you "wash someone's feet" today?

Day 6: John 13:15-17

1. What word or phrase stands out to you from this passage? Why?
2. What does Jesus say will happen if we follow his example in this passage?
3. Spend time today thinking about the blessings that come from serving others.

Day 7: John 13:1-17

Read through the whole passage and write out the verse that spoke to you the most this week. Meditate on that verse today—and for an extra challenge, memorize it!

From *Studies on the Go* by Laurie Polich. Permission granted to reproduce this page for use in buyer's youth group only. Copyright 2006, Youth Specialties.

20. TESTS OF LOYALTY

John 13:18-38

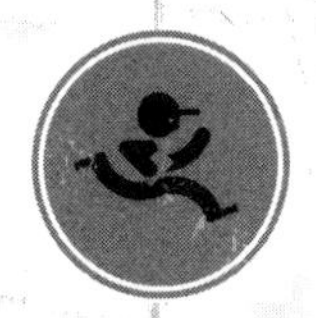

Overview: Jesus predicts both a betrayal and a denial in this passage. The difference is how they are played out. Your students will learn from this passage that we are weak, but he is strong. And our faith must rely on Jesus' strength rather than our own.

After Judas leaves to betray Jesus, Jesus announces to the disciples that he will be going somewhere they cannot go. Peter blurts out, "Lord, why can't I follow you now? I will lay down my life for you." (v. 37) We can imagine Peter was sincere with this brave statement of loyalty. But his pride must have been shattered when Jesus counters him with the truth: "Before the rooster crows, you will disown me three times!" (v. 38)

Peter meant his words when he said them. But like many of us, he doesn't have the strength to live them out. In this session your students will reflect on their own promises—and they'll be comforted by the fact that Jesus' love isn't dependent on our faithfulness to him. It rests on *his* faithfulness to us.

Peter will learn this when he does the very thing he said he'd never do. Sadly, Judas will not. Jesus' grace is available to all. The only thing we have to do is accept it.

SHARE

Warm-Up Qs

1. What's the difference between betrayal and denial? Which do you think is worse?
2. Who is your most loyal friend? How does he or she show loyalty to you?
3. Is there anyone for whom you would lay down your life? If so, who?

OBSERVE

Observation Qs

4. Read John 13:18-30. What prophecy does Jesus give in this passage? Why does he say he gives this prophecy? (v. 19)
5. How does Jesus identify his betrayer? (v. 26) Does he tell all his disciples who it is? If not, to whom does he reveal it?
6. Read vv. 34-35. What "new command" does Jesus give in this passage? What does he say will happen if the disciples fulfill this command?
7. What does Peter say he will do for Jesus? (v. 37) What does Jesus say Peter will do? (v. 38)

THINK

Interpretation Qs

8. As you look at vv. 25-30, do you think the disciples understood that Judas was the betrayer? (Give reasons for your response.)
9. When v. 27 says that Satan entered Judas, does that mean Judas wasn't responsible for his actions? Why or why not?
10. What do you think Jesus means in v. 36? How would the disciples follow him later?
11. Why do you think Peter made such a big promise to Jesus in v. 37? Do you think he meant it? Why or why not?

APPLY

Application Qs

12. To whom do you relate most in this passage—Judas, Peter, or the disciples? Why?
13. Have you ever betrayed someone? Have you ever been betrayed by someone? Which, in your opinion, is worse?
14. Are you the type to make big promises (like Peter) and have trouble fulfilling them? Or do you avoid making promises because you are afraid you won't fulfill them?
15. What do you think it means to deny Jesus? Have you ever done it? If so, when?

DO

Optional Activity:

1	2	3	4	5	6	7	8	9	10
Disloyal							Extremely Loyal		

Create a "Scale of Loyalty" (like the one above) and pass one out to each person in your group. Have them place an X where they are and a circle where they would like to be. Go around and have everyone share why they placed themselves where they did and what changes would need to happen for them to be where they want to be.

Day 1: John 13:18-19

1. What word or phrase stands out to you from these verses? Why?
2. What is Jesus' purpose for prophesying in this passage?
3. Spend time today thinking about how the Bible gives us clues about what is going to happen—and how this helps us live our faith.

Day 2: John 13:20-22

1. What word or phrase stands out to you from this passage? Why?
2. How do the disciples respond to what Jesus says about being betrayed?
3. Spend time today thinking about how you would have responded to Jesus if you were with him in this passage.

Day 3: John 13:23-27

1. What word or phrase stands out to you from this passage? Why?
2. What happens to Judas after he takes the bread?
3. Spend time today thinking about how you feel when you're about to betray Jesus. Does it feel like there's another force at work in you?

Day 4: John 13:28-30

1. What word or phrase stands out to you from this passage? Why?
2. How is the appearance different from the reality in these verses?
3. Spend time today thinking about the things you do that you know are wrong but are hidden to everyone else.

Day 5: John 13:31-35

1. What word or phrase stands out to you from this passage? Why?
2. How will people know we are Jesus' disciples?
3. Spend time today thinking about how many people know you are a follower of Christ. Do they know by your words or by your actions?

Day 6: John 13:36-38

1. What word or phrase stands out to you from this passage? Why?
2. How does Peter's assessment of himself differ from Jesus' assessment of him?
3. Spend time today thinking about whether Jesus' assessment of you would be different from your assessment of yourself. If so, what would the difference be?

Day 7: John 13:18-38

Read through the whole passage and write out the verse that spoke to you the most this week. Meditate on that verse today—and for an extra challenge, memorize it!

From *Studies on the Go* by Laurie Polich. Permission granted to reproduce this page for use in buyer's youth group only. Copyright 2006, Youth Specialties.

21. THE ONLY WAY

John 14:1-14

Overview: Jesus says, "I am the way and the truth and the life. No one comes to the Father except through me." (v. 6) For your students this kind of exclusivity isn't popular; most people around them believe there are many ways to God. But this passage emphasizes that Jesus is the *only* way. Our choice is to reject or accept his claims.

Jesus' death and resurrection provide the only avenue for us to know God, because it is through his death that our sins are forgiven. Jesus reconciled us to God when he died for those things that separated us. That's why he is the only way.

The disciples are confused in this passage because they want to go with Jesus when he goes to the Father. Jesus explains that they need to go *through* him instead. He will have to die to make that possible. That's why he must go before them.

Naturally they don't fully comprehend what he's talking about—but they will. After Jesus' death and resurrection, they'll understand his words through his actions. No other religion has a leader who left an empty grave. That's why there is no other way.

SHARE

Warm-Up Qs

1. If someone said, "There are many ways to get to God," how would you respond?
2. When you're afraid, where do you go for comfort? Is there a person to whom you turn? If so, who?
3. Do you believe God can do great things through people? If so, what kind of people does he choose?

OBSERVE

Observation Qs

4. Read John 14:1-4. What does Jesus tell his disciples to do so they won't be afraid? (v. 1) What does Jesus say he's going to do for them?
5. Read vv. 5-7. What does Thomas ask Jesus? Does Jesus answer his question? What does he say?
6. Read vv. 8-14. What does Philip say to Jesus? (v. 8) How is Jesus' response similar to what he says to Thomas? (vv. 6-7) How is it different?
7. What does Jesus say will happen after he goes to the Father? (v. 12) Who will be able to do great things after that? What are the conditions?

THINK

Interpretation Qs

8. In vv. 2-4, Jesus says he is going to his Father's house. What do you think he means? Is he speaking literally or figuratively?
9. What do you think Jesus is saying in v. 6? Can people get to God without going through Jesus?
10. How is v. 10 possible? Can Jesus and God be one person? If so, how?

11. Look at Jesus' promise in vv. 13-14. Do you think Jesus is saying he will do whatever people ask him to do? If not, which things will he do?

APPLY

Application Qs

12. If you were with the disciples and Jesus said, "Anyone who has seen me has seen the Father," (v. 9) how would you have felt? What would you have thought of him?
13. If someone asked you if you had to be a Christian to get to heaven, based on this passage, how would you respond?
14. Do you feel like you're able to do great things for God? If so, what? If not, why not?
15. Look at Jesus' promise in v. 14. Do you think this promise is for us today? Are there conditions to this promise? If so, what are they?

DO

Optional Activity: Bring some ice in a cup to your group and make sure everyone sees it. Then let it melt (while your group is meeting). At the end, ask them if what's in the cup now is the same as what was in the cup at the beginning of the meeting. Ask them if they see an analogy between the water and ice, and God and Jesus. (Different forms of the same substance.)

Day 1: John 14:1-2

1. What word or phrase stands out to you from these verses? Why?
2. According to Jesus, what helps us not be troubled or afraid?
3. Spend time today thinking about how your trust in God can help you not fear the future.

Day 2: John 14:3-4

1. What word or phrase stands out to you from these verses? Why?
2. What does Jesus say he's going to do for the disciples?
3. Spend time today thinking about how you feel about Jesus' return. Does it excite you or scare you?

Day 3: John 14:5-6

1. What word or phrase stands out to you from these verses? Why?
2. How do we find the way to God?
3. Spend time today thinking about whether or not you truly believe Jesus is the only way to God. How does this verse affect your beliefs?

Day 4: John 14:7-9

1. What word or phrase stands out to you from this passage? Why?
2. How does Philip misunderstand Jesus? Do you think you would have misunderstood him, too?
3. Spend time today thinking about what Jesus says about himself in this passage, and whether or not people think of Jesus and God as one and the same.

Day 5: John 14:10-11

1. What word or phrase stands out to you from these verses? Why?
2. What do we learn about Jesus' identity in these verses?
3. Spend time today thinking about how God's work is carried out through Jesus.

Day 6: John 14:12-14

1. What word or phrase stands out to you from this passage? Why?
2. What is the condition for getting what we ask from Jesus?
3. Spend time today thinking about what it means to ask for something "in Jesus' name." How does it change our prayers?

Day 7: John 14:1-14

Read through the whole passage and write out the verse that spoke to you the most this week. Meditate on that verse today—and for an extra challenge, memorize it!

From *Studies on the Go* by Laurie Polich. Permission granted to reproduce this page for use in buyer's youth group only. Copyright 2006, Youth Specialties.

22. THE HELPER

John 14:15-31 (also 16:5-16)

Overview: Jesus says, "If anyone loves me, he will obey my teaching." (John 14:23) But he knows we can't do it without his help. In this session your students will learn that our help comes in the form of the Holy Spirit. He's the one who brings God's presence to our lives.

Jesus explains that the Holy Spirit comes from the Father, just as he comes from the Father—and comes to change our hearts. Your students might not be able to see him, but they can feel his effects. Every time they are tempted to do something wrong, or moved to do something right, chances are the Spirit is at work. This passage helps us identify his presence.

The Holy Spirit makes our hearts Christ's home. That's what your students will learn in this passage. The Holy Spirit comes alongside us as a counselor, comforter, and friend. And through these functions, we are brought closer to God.

The Holy Spirit helps us turn what we believe into what we live. That's what being a Christian is all about.

SHARE

Warm-Up Qs

1. What do you picture when you think of the Holy Spirit? Why?
2. When you're tempted to do something wrong, do you ever feel a battle inside of you? If so, what does the battle feel like? Who or what do you think it's between?
3. Have you ever experienced God's presence? If so, when? What was it like?

OBSERVE

Observation Qs

4. Read John 14:15-21. What two things does Jesus call the Holy Spirit? (vv. 16-17) Where does he say the Spirit will live?
5. Read vv. 22-31. How does Jesus say we show our love for him? (v. 23) What does he say will be the result?
6. What does Jesus say the Holy Spirit will do for the disciples? (vv. 26-27) (List all the things you see in these verses.)
7. Jump ahead and read John 16:5-16. What does Jesus say in this passage about what the Holy Spirit will do? (vv. 8, 13-14) What needs to happen for the Holy Spirit to come? (v. 7)

THINK

Interpretation Qs

8. Why does Jesus refer to the Holy Spirit as the Counselor and the Spirit of truth? (John 14:16-17) What do you think this means?
9. According to vv. 23-24, do you think it's possible to love Jesus and not obey him? Why or why not? What do you think the Holy Spirit's presence has to do with obedience?
10. Look at what Jesus says about the Spirit in v. 17. What do you think he means? If the Spirit is invisible, how do we know he exists?

11. In John 16:8-14, Jesus says the Spirit will convict the world of guilt and sin. What do you think he means? Does this happen before or after people become Christians?

APPLY

Application Qs

12. Have you ever experienced the Holy Spirit guiding you in your life? If so, what did it feel like?
13. Do you think feelings of guilt are the work of the Holy Spirit? Is this just for Christians—or for everyone?
14. How does the Holy Spirit's presence compare with Jesus and God? Are they all the same or different? How have you experienced all three of them?
15. How is the Holy Spirit at work in your life right now? Would you say he is guiding, teaching, reminding, or convicting? Why?

DO

Optional Activity: Remind your group of the last session, where you watched the ice melt into water. Then take some water, put it in a small pot, and boil it. Ask your group to observe and describe what is happening to the water. Is it staying the same? How is it different? Is there any analogy between the steam and the Holy Spirit? If so, what? (As a follow-up to last week, you now have a third form of the same substance.)

Day 1: John 14:15-17

1. What word or phrase stands out to you from this passage? Why?
2. How do we know the Spirit is there if we can't see him?
3. Spend time today thinking about how we have evidence of the Spirit working inside of us.

Day 2: John 14:18-21

1. What word or phrase stands out to you from this passage? Why?
2. How do we show our love for God?
3. Spend time today thinking about how you show your love for God. How can you do that today?

Day 3: John 14:22-24

1. What word or phrase stands out to you from this passage? Why?
2. According to this passage, is it possible to love Jesus and not obey him?
3. Spend time today thinking about how our obedience directly reflects our love for God. How are you doing with this?

Day 4: John 14:25-26

1. What word or phrase stands out to you from these verses? Why?
2. According to these verses, what two things does the Spirit do for us?
3. Spend time today thinking about whether you have more of a need for teaching or reminding from the Holy Spirit.

Day 5: John 14:27

1. What word or phrase stands out to you from this verse? Why?
2. How is God's peace different from the world's peace?
3. Spend time today thinking about whether or not you are experiencing God's peace.

Day 6: John 14:28-31

1. What word or phrase stands out to you from this passage? Why?
2. Why should the disciples be glad Jesus is leaving them and going to the Father?
3. Spend time today thinking about how we have more of Jesus' power through the Spirit than we would if he were with us in the flesh.

Day 7: John 14:15-31

Read through the whole passage and write out the verse that spoke to you the most this week. Meditate on that verse today—and for an extra challenge, memorize it!

From *Studies on the Go* by Laurie Polich. Permission granted to reproduce this page for use in buyer's youth group only. Copyright 2006, Youth Specialties.

23. THE VINE AND THE BRANCHES

John 15:1-27

Overview: Too often as Christians we try to do Christ's work for him. This passage teaches that we are supposed to do Christ's work *with* him. Cults are formed by people who start following God then end up trying to *be* God instead. The results are just what Jesus predicted in this passage.

Jesus tells a parable about a vine and some branches to illustrate our need to stay attached to him. It will also show your students how he works in our lives. When we bear fruit, Jesus prunes us so we can bear more fruit. It's painful, but it's the way we grow. Our maturity as Christians depends on our trust and connection to the Vine.

Through Jesus we can love with supernatural power. Through Jesus we can teach great truth. Through Jesus we can experience great joy. But the secret to these things is that they only happen *through Jesus.*

Jesus says, "Apart from me you can do nothing," (v. 5) and history has shown it to be true. People have died following leaders who cut themselves off from Jesus. Staying connected to him is what gives us life.

SHARE

Warm-Up Qs

1. What does it mean to "prune" a tree? Have you ever done it (or seen it done)? If so, what is the process?
2. Do you think it's possible to cut off a branch from a plant or tree and keep it alive? If so, how? If not, why not?
3. What is the greatest extent someone has gone to show you that he or she loved you? What is the greatest extent you have gone to show you loved someone else?

OBSERVE

Observation Qs

4. Read John 15:1-8. How does Jesus describe himself in this passage? How does he describe the Father? How does he describe his disciples?
5. What happens to branches that do not bear fruit? (v. 2) What happens to branches that do bear fruit? What does it take for a branch to bear fruit? (v. 4)
6. Read vv. 9-17. How does Jesus say we remain in his love? (v. 10) What command does he give? (v. 12) What example does he give of this command? (v. 13)
7. Read vv. 18-20. How does Jesus describe the connection he has with the disciples? How does the world relate to both of them?

THINK

Interpretation Qs

8. What do you think Jesus means when he says branches that don't bear fruit will be cut off? (v. 2) What do you think he means when he says branches that do bear fruit will be pruned?

9. Who do you think are the branches in this passage? Are they just his disciples or all his followers? How do "branches" become disconnected from the vine (or Jesus)?
10. Look at v. 12. Why do you think Jesus only gives this one commandment? Do you think v. 13 refers more to him or to us? Why?
11. What do you think Jesus means in v. 16 when he says his disciples will bear "fruit that will last"? What would be an example of this fruit?

APPLY

Application Qs

12. If you were a branch on Jesus' vine, what would you look like? Would you be fruitful and thriving or empty and brittle? Why?
13. Have you ever felt "pruned" by God so you could bear more fruit? If so, how?
14. Do you consider yourself to be God's friend? If not, why not? If so, what are some of the ways you show your friendship to him?
15. Have you ever experienced people not liking you (or alienating you) because you were a Christian? If so, when? If not, have you ever seen it happen to someone else?

DO

Optional Activity: Find a fruit tree (or bush) that is accessible to your group. Before or after this study, have your group spend 10 minutes in silence studying the plant and writing down their observations. (Here are some questions to get them started: Where is the most fruit? Where is least fruit? What part of the tree looks the healthiest? What part of the tree is the least healthy? Are there any fallen branches? Do they have fruit? etc.) Have them share their findings with the group.

Day 1: John 15:1-4

1. What word or phrase stands out to you from this passage? Why?
2. According to this passage, what happens to us if we bear fruit for Christ? What do you think this means?
3. Spend time today thinking about how God might be pruning you to bear more fruit.

Day 2: John 15:5-8

1. What word or phrase stands out to you from this passage? Why?
2. What do you think it means to stay connected to the vine? What happens when we don't stay connected?
3. Spend time today thinking about the ways you can stay connected to Christ in your day-to-day life.

Day 3: John 15:9-13

1. What word or phrase stands out to you from this passage? Why?
2. What command does Jesus give us in this passage? How can we do this?
3. Spend time today thinking about specific ways you can fulfill Christ's command.

Day 4: John 15:14-17

1. What word or phrase stands out to you from this passage? Why?
2. Why does Jesus call us friends? How do we show our friendship to Christ?
3. Spend time today thinking about whether your relationships with others reflect your relationship with God.

Day 5: John 15:18-21

1. What word or phrase stands out to you from this passage? Why?
2. How do our sufferings relate to Christ's sufferings?
3. Spend time today thinking about how you can have a different attitude about suffering, knowing your suffering can be a witness for Christ.

Day 6: John 15:22-27

1. What word or phrase stands out to you from this passage? Why?
2. Why does Jesus say the people who have seen him and don't believe are guilty?
3. Spend time today thinking about how we are accountable for what we know, not for what we don't know.

Day 7: John 15:1-27

Read through the whole passage and write out the verse that spoke to you the most this week. Meditate on that verse today—and for an extra challenge, memorize it!

From *Studies on the Go* by Laurie Polich. Permission granted to reproduce this page for use in buyer's youth group only. Copyright 2006, Youth Specialties.

24. PAIN THAT LEADS TO JOY

John 16:16-33

Overview: Childbirth is the most excruciating pain anyone can experience. But any mother will tell you the pain is miraculously forgotten the second the baby comes out. Jesus uses this analogy to describe what's going to happen to the disciples when he is taken away. Their joy will be greater when they see him because of the pain they endured.

Your students have probably experienced this to some degree. The more pain they endure in their studying, the more joy they'll experience in their future. Short-term pain produces long-term pleasure. And the pleasure is sweeter when you go through pain.

Jesus says, "In this world you will have trouble." (v. 33) Things happen that make us wonder if God cares. People we love die. Parents we love get divorced. Relationships we love are broken. It's easy to want to give up.

But if we endure our pain, we'll discover that the trouble we have in this world is not permanent. God has a purpose in everything. In the last verse of this passage, Jesus says he has overcome the world. Soon he will go on to prove it.

SHARE
Warm-Up Qs

1. Someone once said, "Short-term pleasure brings long-term pain, while short-term pain brings long-term pleasure." Do you agree with this statement?
2. What do an athlete, a student, and a pregnant woman all have in common?
3. Have you ever been willing to go through pain to get something you wanted? If so, when?

OBSERVE
Observation Qs

4. Read John 16:16-24. What does Jesus tell his disciples that they don't understand? (vv. 16-18) Where is he going? When will the disciples see him?
5. What does Jesus say will happen to the disciples? (v. 20) What illustration does Jesus give in v. 21 to describe the disciples' pain?
6. Read vv. 25-33. How does Jesus say he has been speaking? (v. 25) Why do the disciples understand him better now? (v. 29) What do they say about Jesus' knowledge? What does it cause them to do? (v. 30)
7. What does Jesus say the disciples will do to him? (v. 32) How does he comfort them in spite of what they will do? What does Jesus say they will experience? (v. 33)

THINK
Interpretation Qs

8. Why are the disciples confused at the beginning of the passage? Do you think Jesus cleared it up for them in vv. 19-20? Why or why not?

9. Why do you think Jesus uses childbirth as an illustration for what's going to happen to the disciples? What parallels do you see between them?
10. What do you think Jesus means when he says the disciples can ask for anything in his name and receive it? (vv. 23-24) What does it mean to ask for something in Jesus' name?
11. In v. 33, Jesus says the disciples will have peace in spite of the world's trouble. What do you think this means? How is it possible to have peace when there is trouble?

APPLY

Application Qs

12. Has God ever allowed you to go through pain? If so, when? Do you look back on it differently now?
13. Do you think prayers in Jesus' name are different from other prayers? If so, how? Does God always answer them?
14. Have you ever had the experience of not understanding something Jesus said (in the Bible), and then understanding it later? If so, what made the difference?
15. At the end of this passage Jesus talks about a peace you can have in the midst of trouble. Have you ever experienced this? If so, when?

DO

Optional Activity: Try an object lesson. Show your group the difference between a thermostat and a thermometer. (A thermostat sets the temperature in the room while a thermometer reflects the temperature of the room.) Ask them which they are more like in their faith—a thermometer that goes up and down depending on the circumstances, or a thermostat that stays steady in the midst of all circumstances. Affirm at the end that the peace Jesus describes in this chapter is more like a thermostat.

Day 1: John 16:1-7

1. What word or phrase stands out to you from this passage? Why?
2. How does Jesus comfort the disciples in this passage?
3. Spend time today thinking about the way God comforts you with his promises.

Day 2: John 16:8-15

1. What word or phrase stands out to you from this passage? Why?
2. What does Jesus say the Holy Spirit will do for us?
3. Spend time today thinking about how you have experienced the Holy Spirit in the ways Jesus describes in this passage.

Day 3: John 16:16-20

1. What word or phrase stands out to you from this passage? Why?
2. How does Jesus prepare the disciples for what's about to happen?
3. Spend time today thinking about how prepared you are for the end of your life. How do Jesus' words strengthen you for what's to come?

Day 4: John 16:21-24

1. What word or phrase stands out to you from this passage? Why?
2. How does Jesus use the illustration of childbirth to give the disciples hope?
3. Spend time today thinking about how God's blessings usually come with pain. Have you ever experienced this in your life?

Day 5: John 16:25-30

1. What word or phrase stands out to you from this passage? Why?
2. How does Jesus change his style of speech in this passage?
3. Spend time today thinking about the different styles of communication Jesus uses and why it's important to know this in order to understand God's Word.

Day 6: John 16:31-33

1. What word or phrase stands out to you from this passage? Why?
2. What does Jesus say the disciples will do to him? Why does he tell them this?
3. Spend time today thinking about how God's faithfulness to you is bigger than your faithfulness to him and how this can give you peace.

Day 7: John 16:1-33

Read through the whole passage and write out the verse that spoke to you the most this week. Meditate on that verse today—and for an extra challenge, memorize it!

From *Studies on the Go* by Laurie Polich. Permission granted to reproduce this page for use in buyer's youth group only. Copyright 2006, Youth Specialties.

25. JESUS' PRAYER FOR US

John 17:1-26

Overview: In this prayer we get an inside look at Jesus' relationship with the Father. It's kind of like eavesdropping on a conversation between friends. Right from the start we see that Jesus and God share in the same glory. As the prayer goes on, the intimacy of their relationship is revealed.

On the cross Jesus will appear to be far from God's love. But here Jesus affirms that he's in the center of God's love. This will teach your students that God's love is not manifested through protecting us from difficulty. It's manifested in helping us overcome difficulty with his strength. That's what Jesus will experience on the cross—and he prays for that same strength in us.

Ultimately Jesus knows God's love won't protect him from the world. But it will empower him to overcome the world. This is the love he prays for in his disciples. It's also the love he prays for in us. It's God's simple strategy to change the world. And Jesus' prayer is for us to accomplish it.

SHARE

Warm-Up Qs

1. If you knew you had three days left to live, what would you do?
2. If you could ask God to do anything for the people you love, what would you ask him to do?
3. If you knew Jesus prayed for you, what do you think he would pray?

OBSERVE

Observation Qs

4. Read John 17:1-5. What does Jesus ask God to do for him? What does he say he has done for God?
5. Read vv. 6-19. What does Jesus say about his disciples? (vv. 7-8) What does he pray for them? (v. 11) What does he say about the one who was lost? (v. 12)
6. Read vv. 20-26. Who is this prayer for? (v. 20) How is this prayer similar to his prayer for the disciples? How is it different?
7. What does Jesus say in v. 26? How is this a prayer for Jesus' work in the future?

THINK

Interpretation Qs

8. In v. 4, Jesus says he has brought God glory by completing the work he gave him to do. What do you think this work is? How did he complete it?
9. When Jesus prays for his disciples, he says glory has come to him through them. (v. 10) What do you think this means? Is it related to the glory he brought to God? If so, how?
10. Why does Jesus tell God not to take the disciples out of the world? (v. 15) Why is it necessary for the disciples to stay in

the world? Why does Jesus pray that they will be sanctified? (v. 17)

11. Look at what Jesus prays for all believers in v. 21. Do you think this prayer has been answered? Why or why not?

APPLY

Application Qs

12. When Jesus prays for himself, he says that God granted him authority to give people eternal life. (v. 2) Do we have a part in that process? If so, what?
13. According to this prayer, what do you think it means to glorify God? How do we do it? Do you feel like you are glorifying God?
14. What do you think it means to be sanctified? (v. 17) Do you think you are sanctified? Why or why not?
15. Look at Jesus' prayer for you in vv. 20-26. What part of this prayer do you need the most? Why?

DO

Optional Activity: Have your group write a prayer following Jesus' outline. Let them spread out around the room with paper and pens (or notebooks), and give them 10 minutes to write a prayer for themselves, 10 minutes to write a prayer for their friends and families, and 10 minutes to write a prayer for the world.

Day 1: John 17:1-5

1. What word or phrase stands out to you from this passage? Why?
2. According to this passage, how did Jesus bring God glory?
3. Spend time today thinking about how Jesus' work on earth brought glory to God.

Day 2: John 17:6-10

1. What word or phrase stands out to you from this passage? Why?
2. What does Jesus say about the disciples in these verses? How have they brought glory to Jesus?
3. Spend time today thinking about how people bring glory to Jesus when they show themselves to be his disciples. How have you done this?

Day 3: John 17:11-12

1. What word or phrase stands out to you from these verses? Why?
2. What does Jesus pray for his disciples in these verses?
3. Spend time today thinking about the things Jesus prays for his disciples, and what that might mean for us.

Day 4: John 17:13-19

1. What word or phrase stands out to you from this passage? Why?
2. Why doesn't Jesus pray for his disciples to be taken from the world? Why do you think he wants them to stay even though he knows it will be difficult?
3. Spend time today thinking about what it means to be in this world but not of this world.

Day 5: John 17:20-23

1. What word or phrase stands out to you from this passage? Why?
2. Do you think you're one of the ones Christ is praying for in this passage? Why or why not?
3. Spend time today thinking about whether or not you think Christ's prayer (for all believers) has been answered. What would the world look like if it were?

Day 6: John 17:24-26

1. What word or phrase stands out to you from this passage? Why?
2. What does Jesus pray about his presence in our lives? Have you experienced this?
3. Spend time today thinking about how Christ's presence in your life makes your life different.

Day 7: John 17:1-26

Read through the whole passage and write out the verse that spoke to you the most this week. Meditate on that verse today—and for an extra challenge, memorize it!

From *Studies on the Go* by Laurie Polich. Permission granted to reproduce this page for use in buyer's youth group only. Copyright 2006, Youth Specialties.

26. ABANDONED AND ACCUSED

John 18:1-40

Overview: Just five chapters earlier, Peter said to Jesus, "I will lay down my life for you." (John 13:37) Now he can't even admit that he knows him. It's hard to imagine how Peter can go so quickly in this passage from ace disciple to non-disciple...until we look at ourselves.

Ironically it tends to happen after the times we feel closest to God. Days after saying we're going to change the world for Christ, we find we can't even stand up for him. It gives us a little more grace when we look at Peter in this story.

When Peter heard the rooster crow, he must have felt guilt and despair. At some point your students may have felt the same way. But the good news is, even if Peter was too weak to hold on to Christ, Christ's love wouldn't let go of Peter. And that love will prove strong enough to bring Peter back.

Abandoned by his friends, Jesus now faces a man who can't decide what to do with him. And we'll see in the next chapter that this man isn't strong enough to set Jesus free. As the crowd shouts, "Give us Barabbas," (v. 40) it's apparent Jesus will not be spared his destiny. And that destiny would lead him to the cross.

SHARE
Warm-Up Qs

1. Have you ever been wrongly accused of something? If so, when? What ended up happening?
2. Have you (or one of your friends) ever done anything that created distance in your friendship? If so, how did it affect you? How did it affect your friend?
3. When was the last time you remember feeling alone or abandoned? What were the circumstances that made you feel this way?

OBSERVE
Observation Qs

4. Read John 18:1-11. Who comes after Jesus? After he identifies himself, what happens? (v. 6) What does Peter do to try to protect Jesus? (v. 10)
5. Read vv. 12-27. Where is Jesus taken? (v. 12) What happens to him while the high priest questions him? (v. 22) What's the official's reason for treating him this way?
6. How many times does Peter get asked if he knows Jesus? Who are two of the people who ask him? (vv. 17, 26) What happens after Peter's third response? (v. 27)
7. Read vv. 28-40. How does Jesus respond when Pilate questions him about being a king? (v. 34) Who does Jesus say ultimately listens to him? (v. 37)

THINK
Interpretation Qs

8. Look at how Jesus responds to Peter after he tried to protect him. (v. 11) What does Jesus mean about drinking the cup the Father gave him?

9. Why do you think Peter denied that he knew Jesus after trying to protect him with his sword? What do you think changed him?
10. Why do you think Pilate tried to get the Jews to take responsibility for Jesus' judgment? (v. 31) Do you think Pilate was afraid? Why or why not?
11. When Jesus describes his kingdom in v. 36, do you think it sounds more or less powerful than an earthly kingdom? Why?

APPLY

Application Qs

12. To whom do you relate more in this passage, Peter or Pilate? Why?
13. Have you ever been embarrassed about your relationship with God? If so, when? Is your relationship with God ever affected by what others think?
14. If someone asked you to describe God's kingdom, how would you describe it? Is it something you can see? Where is it? What is it like?
15. Where is it hardest for you to live out your faith—at home, at school, or with your friends? Why?

DO

Optional Activity: Over the next week have your group keep a chart of how many times they stand up for Christ and how many times they deny they know him (in their words, their actions, or their silence). Have them spend five minutes at the end of each day reflecting on conversations, classes, recreational activities, and family time—and keep track of their successes and failures.

Day 1: John 18:1-11

1. What word or phrase stands out to you from this passage? Why?
2. How does Peter try to protect Jesus in this passage? Why does Jesus reject his protection?
3. Spend time today thinking about how God's agenda is different from ours, and how we are called to submit to God's plan.

Day 2: John 18:12-18

1. What word or phrase stands out to you from this passage? Why?
2. Why do you think Peter denied that he was with Jesus? Why was he afraid to admit it?
3. Spend time today thinking about the times you are embarrassed to admit that you're a Christian. What causes you to be embarrassed?

Day 3: John 18:19-24

1. What word or phrase stands out to you from this passage? Why?
2. Do you think the officials felt threatened by Jesus in this passage? Why did they strike him?
3. Spend time today thinking about what makes Jesus intimidating to people who don't follow him.

Day 4: John 18:25-27

1. What word or phrase stands out to you from this passage? Why?
2. How do you think Peter felt when he heard the rooster crow? Have you ever felt that way?
3. Spend time today thinking about times you haven't stood up for your faith and felt bad about it afterward. How can you stand up for your faith today?

Day 5: John 18:28-32

1. What word or phrase stands out to you from this passage? Why?
2. Why do you think Pilate tried to give Jesus back to the Jews to decide his fate?
3. Spend time today thinking about the ways we avoid responsibility for difficult decisions.

Day 6: John 18:33-40

1. What word or phrase stands out to you from this passage? Why?
2. How do you see Pilate struggle in this passage? Why do you think he was struggling?
3. Spend time today thinking about what you would have done if you were in Pilate's position.

Day 7: John 18:1-40

Read through the whole passage and write out the verse that spoke to you the most this week. Meditate on that verse today—and for an extra challenge, memorize it!

From *Studies on the Go* by Laurie Polich. Permission granted to reproduce this page for use in buyer's youth group only. Copyright 2006, Youth Specialties.

27. DECISION DILEMMA

John 19:1-22

Overview: There are many people who don't say no to Jesus, but they never say yes, either. Pontius Pilate is one of them. His story shows us that when it comes to Jesus Christ, no decision *is* a decision. And sometimes it's the worst kind of decision there is.

Three times Jesus is proclaimed innocent. Then he's sentenced to death. The interrogation that began in the last chapter ends with Pilate finding no basis for a charge. Yet the crowd shouts, "Crucify him!" And Pilate shouts back, "You crucify him!"

Nobody wanted to take responsibility for his death. There was a sense that they knew something big was going to happen. They were right. Jesus was about to die for no crime, so he could die for every crime. He was going to do this for us all.

Pilate could never say Jesus wasn't the Christ. It was because he couldn't stand up and say Jesus *was* the Christ that Jesus' fate was sealed. For all time Pilate would be remembered as the one who sentenced Christ to death.

The story of Pontius Pilate shows your students that when it comes to Jesus, we all have to take a stand. When we don't, we may find ourselves taking one anyway.

SHARE
Warm-Up Qs

1. Someone once said "No decision is a decision." Do you agree with this statement? Why or why not?
2. How much of our lives do you think is planned by God—and how much of our lives is planned by us?
3. When you think of Pontius Pilate, what is the first word that comes to your mind? Why?

OBSERVE
Observation Qs

4. Read John 19:1-16. When Pilate gives Jesus to the soldiers, how do they dress him? (v. 2) Where do they strike him? What do they call him?
5. What does Pilate keep trying to do in this passage? (vv. 4, 5, 6) What does the crowd keep yelling at him? What makes Pilate afraid? (vv. 7-8)
6. What does Pilate say to Jesus to try to get him to talk? (v. 10) How does Jesus respond? What happens when Pilate tries to set Jesus free? (v. 12)
7. Read vv. 17-22. What notice does Pilate fasten to the cross? What do the chief priests say about it? How does Pilate respond?

THINK
Interpretation Qs

8. Why do you think Pilate kept trying to hand Jesus over to the Jews? Why didn't he handle Jesus himself?
9. What ultimately causes Pilate to cave in to the Jews request? (vv. 12-13) What does this tell you about Pilate?
10. Look at what Jesus says in v. 11. What do you think he means? Was Pilate responsible for what was happening? Why or why not?

11. Look at what the Jews want Pilate to write on the notice. (v. 21) Since Pilate has already given in to have Jesus crucified, why doesn't he give in to this? What do you think Pilate was feeling (based on his behavior in this passage)?

APPLY

Application Qs

12. Have you ever had to stand against the crowd to do what you knew was right? What did you end up doing? How did it feel?
13. Have you ever been in a position where you had to choose whether or not to stick up for a friend (who was being talked about or criticized)? What did you end up doing? Why?
14. Do you think it's possible to be prevented from doing the right thing, or is it always by choice? (Give reasons for your response.)
15. Where in your life do you need to take a stronger stand when it comes to your relationship with God? Which "crowd" is the hardest one for you to deal with?

DO

Optional Activity: Get a copy of the Nicene Creed for your group. (You can find a copy via an Internet search.) Explain to your group that early Christians wrote it around AD 325 to unify them and reaffirm what they believed. Ask your students to look for the name Pontius Pilate in the creed. They will see that he's the only one listed for the suffering of Jesus. Talk about the fact that no decision is a decision...especially when it comes to Pontius Pilate.

Day 1: John 19:1-3

1. What word or phrase stands out to you from this passage? Why?
2. How do the soldiers treat Jesus in these verses? How does Jesus respond?
3. Spend time today thinking about the strength that we display when we refrain from fighting back.

Day 2: John 19:4-6

1. What word or phrase stands out to you from this passage? Why?
2. How does Pilate try to absolve himself from sentencing Jesus in this passage?
3. Spend time today thinking about a time you were with people doing something you felt was wrong, and whether or not you tried to get out of it.

Day 3: John 19:7-9

1. What word or phrase stands out to you from this passage? Why?
2. Why is Pilate afraid in this passage? Would you have been afraid in his position?
3. Spend time today thinking about the need for all people to decide whether or not Jesus is the Son of God.

Day 4: John 19:10-11

1. What word or phrase stands out to you from these verses? Why?
2. Where does Pilate's power to determine Jesus' destiny come from? What does that tell you about God's ultimate control?
3. Spend time today thinking about the fact that nothing happens that can stop God's plan and purposes in this world.

Day 5: John 19:12-13

1. What word or phrase stands out to you from these verses? Why?
2. What do the Jews say in these verses that ultimately stops Pilate from setting Jesus free?
3. Spend time today thinking about whether you care more about what others think or about what God thinks.

Day 6: John 19:14-16

1. What word or phrase stands out to you from this passage? Why?
2. What does Pilate keep calling Jesus to the people? How do they respond?
3. Spend time today thinking about whether you claim Jesus as your king. How do you show this in your life?

Day 7: John 19:1-22

Read through the whole passage and write out the verse that spoke to you the most this week. Meditate on that verse today—and for an extra challenge, memorize it!

From *Studies on the Go* by Laurie Polich. Permission granted to reproduce this page for use in buyer's youth group only. Copyright 2006, Youth Specialties.

28. THE END...OR IS IT?

John 19:23-42

Overview: In this passage Jesus shows us how much he loves us by reaching out his hands. Then he lets soldiers nail those hands to a cross.

The other Gospels record that when Jesus hung on the cross, people mocked him saying, "He saved others, but he can't save himself!" Yet the irony of that statement is that it was *because* he was saving others that he refrained from saving himself. How tempting it must have been to call on God to spare him. Instead, he humbly submitted to sparing us.

With our sin on his shoulders, Jesus became our ultimate sacrifice. That was the work of the cross. In v. 30, Jesus says, "It is finished." His work was done. Our sin was absolved...and Jesus was dead. Joseph of Arimathea took his body off the cross and placed it in a grave. The tomb was his new home.

It appeared this was the end of the story. Often it feels like that in our lives. But this session shows your students that appearances can be deceiving—especially when it comes to God.

SHARE

Warm-Up Qs

1. When was the last time you saw a movie that had a surprise ending? What did you think was going to happen? Why?
2. Have you ever watched someone suffer? If so, when? How did it make you feel?
3. Who is the closest person to you who has died? How did it affect you?

OBSERVE

Observation Qs

4. Read John 19:23-27. Who is by the cross while Jesus is crucified? (v. 25) What does Jesus say to them?
5. Read vv. 28-37. What does Jesus say in this passage before he dies? What do the soldiers do to Jesus after he dies that's procedurally different? (vv. 32-34) What prophecy does this fulfill? (v. 36-37)
6. Read vv. 38-42. Who asks permission to take Jesus' body? How is he related to Jesus? (v. 38) Who comes with him? (v. 39)
7. What do they do with Jesus' body? What customs do they follow when they wrap the body? (v. 40) Where do they bury him? (v. 41) How many people had been buried in this particular tomb?

THINK

Interpretation Qs

8. When Jesus says, "It is finished," (v. 30) what does he mean?
9. Why do you think Jesus told his mother to receive John as a son? (v. 26) What (if anything) does that tell you about his relationship with her?
10. How many prophecies were fulfilled during the crucifixion account? Why do you think John wrote all of these down?

11. Why do you think Joseph and Nicodemus came for Jesus' body? Why didn't Jesus' disciples come? Where do you think they were?

APPLY

Application Qs

12. If you were one of the 12 disciples, how would you feel now that Jesus was dead? Would you be more sad or disappointed? Why?
13. If you were around when Jesus was being crucified, would you have been at the cross mourning (like the four women) or away from the cross (like the disciples)? Why?
14. Have you ever experienced a time when it seemed like God was asleep or even dead? If so, when? What did it feel like?
15. What feelings do you have when you think about what Christ went through on that cross? Do you feel grateful? Upset? Sad? Angry? Guilty? Relieved? Do you feel like he did it for you? Why or why not?

DO

Optional Activity: Rent *The Passion of the Christ* and watch the crucifixion scene with your small group. Give your students 10 minutes of silence to think, pray, write, and reflect, and then go around your group and have the students share their reflections on how the scene made them feel.

Day 1: John 19:17-22

1. What word or phrase stands out to you from this passage? Why?
2. What words does Pilate write to be put on Jesus' cross? How is he stronger in his decision in this chapter than in the previous chapter?
3. Spend time today thinking about how Jesus died as a king for people who didn't acknowledge his kingship.

Day 2: John 19:23-27

1. What word or phrase stands out to you from this passage? Why?
2. How does Jesus show tenderness to his mother in this passage?
3. Spend time today thinking about how Jesus had the time to care for individuals, while he was dying for the whole world.

Day 3: John 19:28-30

1. What word or phrase stands out to you from this passage? Why?
2. What are Jesus' last words on the cross? What do you think they meant?
3. Spend time today thinking about how Jesus' death completed the sentence for our sin.

Day 4: John 19:31-37

1. What word or phrase stands out to you from this passage? Why?
2. What Old Testament prophecies are fulfilled in this passage? How are they fulfilled?
3. Spend time today thinking about how many Old Testament prophecies were fulfilled by Jesus—and how this can strengthen your faith in him.

Day 5: John 19:38-39

1. What word or phrase stands out to you from these verses? Why?
2. What do Joseph of Arimathea and Nicodemus have in common? How do they come out of hiding in this passage as Jesus' disciples?
3. Spend time today thinking about the times you've hid your faith in Jesus, and how you can show your allegiance to him today.

Day 6: John 19:40-42

1. What word or phrase stands out to you from this passage? Why?
2. How does John describe the tomb where Jesus had been laid? Does anything strike you as significant?
3. Spend time today thinking about how you would have felt if you were a follower of Jesus and you had just seen him die.

Day 7: John 19:17-42

Read through the whole passage and write out the verse that spoke to you the most this week. Meditate on that verse today—and for an extra challenge, memorize it!

From *Studies on the Go* by Laurie Polich. Permission granted to reproduce this page for use in buyer's youth group only. Copyright 2006, Youth Specialties.

29. RESURRECTION SIGHTINGS

John 20:1-30

Overview: It's been three days since Jesus was laid in the tomb. But now his body is gone. When Mary discovers the empty tomb, she assumes his body's been stolen. She will soon find out that Jesus left the tomb by himself.

Of course, not everyone believes that. People have developed theories to prove the resurrection never occurred. But this passage reveals that people had separate encounters with the risen Lord. So the question is, were they *all* in on a conspiracy? If so, how did they collaborate on such an elaborate plot?

The body was never found. It was stolen, hidden, or raised from the dead. Jesus' empty grave will lead your students to decide whether or not they believe in the resurrection. Their conclusion will determine their faith.

Without the resurrection, Christianity preaches a prophet and teacher who taught us how to live. With the resurrection, Christianity preaches a Savior who comes to be our Lord. Only one has the power to change lives—and he is the one whom we encounter in this passage.

And he is no longer dead. He's alive!

SHARE

Warm-Up Qs

1. Have you ever thought you'd seen a ghost? If so, when? If not, have you ever been scared that you might see a ghost?
2. If someone who had died could visit you, who would you want it to be?
3. Have you ever wanted to see something so bad that you wondered if you imagined it? If so, when?

OBSERVE

Observation Qs

4. Read John 20:1-18. Who is the first to see that Jesus' body is gone? Who does she tell? Do they believe her?
5. To whom does Jesus appear first? Does she recognize him? What does he tell her to do?
6. Read vv. 19-31. Where are the disciples when Jesus appears to them? What does he show them? (v. 20) What does he give them? (v. 22)
7. Which disciple isn't with the group when Jesus appears to them? (v. 24) Does he believe them? How does Jesus prove himself to this disciple?

THINK

Interpretation Qs

8. Why do you think Mary was the first to see Jesus? Is there any significance in this? Why weren't the disciples the first ones to see him?
9. Why do you think Mary didn't recognize Jesus at first? What caused her to finally recognize him?
10. Look at what Jesus says in v. 19. Why do you think he says this? What does he mean?

11. In v. 29, Jesus says that those who believe without seeing are blessed. Why do you think he says this? Who would fall into this category?

APPLY

Application Qs

12. To whom do you relate most in this chapter—Mary, Thomas, or the rest of the disciples? Why?
13. Have you ever had an experience similar to Mary's, in which Jesus suddenly became real to you? If so, when?
14. From this passage Thomas is often referred to as "Doubting Thomas." Would you say you have more faith than Thomas? Or is your faith similar to his? What would it take for you to increase your faith?
15. Jesus says he is sending the disciples the same way the Father has sent him—with his wounds. (v. 21) In what ways can God use the wounds in our lives to help others? Do you think he could use yours?

DO

Optional Activity: Go around the group and have each of your students share one past hurt which they would be willing to give to God to see if he could use it. After each person shares, have the group repeat Jesus' words in unison: "As the Father has sent me, I am sending you." (v. 21) Close in prayer.

Day 1: John 20:1-9

1. What word or phrase stands out to you from this passage? Why?
2. What do you think Mary and the two disciples thought had happened to Jesus' body? What would you have thought?
3. Spend time today thinking about how we base our assumptions on what we can see, but God often works in the unseen.

Day 2: John 20:10-14

1. What word or phrase stands out to you from this passage? Why?
2. What does Mary see when she looks into the tomb? Do you think she realized what she was seeing?
3. Spend time today thinking about how God may have brought angels to visit you in a form you didn't recognize.

Day 3: John 20:15-18

1. What word or phrase stands out to you from this passage? Why?
2. What is it that causes Mary to recognize Jesus?
3. Spend time today thinking about the times you've recognized God's voice in your life. What is it that causes you to recognize it's him?

Day 4: John 20:19-23

1. What word or phrase stands out to you from this passage? Why?
2. How does Jesus get inside the room where the disciples are? How do you think this affected them?
3. Spend time today thinking about how God gets through the locked doors in your life. Is there a door that's locked right now? If so, what would it take to open it?

Day 5: John 20:24-28

1. What word or phrase stands out to you from this passage? Why?
2. What does Thomas say he'd need in order to believe it was Jesus? How does Jesus respond to him?
3. Spend time today thinking about how Jesus meets us where we are. Does he need to meet a certain friend or family member in your life?

Day 6: John 20:29-31

1. What word or phrase stands out to you from this passage? Why?
2. Whom does Jesus say is blessed in these verses? Do you think that includes you?
3. Spend time today thinking about the blessing you are to God for believing in Jesus without seeing him.

Day 7: John 20:1-31

Read through the whole passage and write out the verse that spoke to you the most this week. Meditate on that verse today—and for an extra challenge, memorize it!

From *Studies on the Go* by Laurie Polich. Permission granted to reproduce this page for use in buyer's youth group only. Copyright 2006, Youth Specialties.

30. RESURRECTED LIFE

John 21:1-25

Overview: The disciples have gone back to fishing. They know Jesus is alive, but they don't know when they'll see him again. A net full of fish causes them to recognize his presence. And they head to the beach for their resurrection meal.

After they eat breakfast, Jesus turns to Peter to restore their relationship. He asks him three times, "Do you love me?" Three affirmations of love replace Peter's three denials. But this time Jesus challenges Peter to translate that love into action.

Each time Peter proclaims his love, Jesus says, "Feed my sheep." But "feeding sheep" will include being led where he doesn't want to go. (v. 18) Peter asks if it will be the same for another disciple, but Jesus tells Peter the only story he will know is his own.

In this passage your students will see that each of us has a story. And it's unlike anyone else's in the world. Jesus will lead us as we step out to live that story. And he has more than this life on earth to see it through.

SHARE

Warm-Up Qs

1. When you're depressed, what do you do to feel better? Does it work?
2. Have you ever been more interested in someone else's life than your own? If so, why?
3. If you had a chance to do something over (or something new) in your life, what would it be?

OBSERVE

Observation Qs

4. Read John 21:1-14. What time of day is it when the disciples go fishing? (v. 3) How long have they been fishing when Jesus calls out to them? (v. 4) What does he tell them to do?
5. When do the disciples figure out that it's Jesus talking to them? (v. 7) How does Peter react? What does Jesus invite the disciples to do?
6. Read vv. 15-25. What does Jesus ask Peter when they're done eating? (v. 15) How many times does he ask? Does Peter's response change? (vv. 15-17) If so, how?
7. What does Jesus say will happen to Peter when he is old? (v. 18) How does Peter respond? (vv. 20-21) What does Jesus say to him? (v. 22)

THINK

Interpretation Qs

8. How do you think the disciples felt when Jesus asked them what they had caught? (v. 5) Do you think they were reluctant to cast their nets on the other side? Why or why not?
9. What do you think it was that made the disciples recognize Jesus?

10. Why does Jesus ask Peter three times if he loves him? (vv. 15-17) Do you think he needed him to answer three times? If so, why?
11. Look at Jesus' words to Peter in v. 22. Do they sound harsh to you? What do you think he means?

APPLY

Application Qs

12. Have you ever felt like you disappointed Jesus? If so, when? What helped you restore your relationship with him?
13. What do vv. 18-22 tell us about God's will for our lives? How do you interpret this for yourself?
14. What has changed in your life as a result of your relationship with God? What still needs to change?
15. Do you feel like you're living God's will for your life or your own will? What needs to change for you to be living a "resurrected life"?

DO

Optional Activity: Pass out seeds to your group and tell your students to plant them, water them, and watch them grow. Tell them to keep a record of what the seeds looked like when they planted them, what they needed to do to nurture their growth, and what they looked like when they came up. Invite them to see this as an object lesson for spiritual growth: When we allow ourselves to die in certain areas of our lives, God brings new growth, and we become new creations. This is a lifelong lesson for them to take with them!

Day 1: John 21:1-3

1. What word or phrase stands out to you from this passage? Why?
2. Why do you think the disciples went fishing after all that had just happened?
3. Spend time today thinking about what you do when you've gone through something difficult, and you need to get away and think.

Day 2: John 21:4-6

1. What word or phrase stands out to you from this passage? Why?
2. How do you think the disciples felt when a stranger told them how to fish? How do you think they felt after their catch?
3. Spend time today thinking about people who offer suggestions that you don't listen to because you think you know better. How might today's reading encourage you to listen?

Day 3: John 21:7-9

1. What word or phrase stands out to you from this passage? Why?
2. How is Peter's reaction to Jesus different from the rest of the disciples' reaction? Would you say you are more like him—or them?
3. Spend time today thinking about how you respond to Jesus. Do you tend to be more spontaneous (act without thinking) or controlled (think without acting)?

Day 4: John 21:10-14

1. What word or phrase stands out to you from this passage? Why?
2. What does Jesus do with the disciples in these verses? Do you think they recognized him by his physical appearance or by his actions? Why?
3. Spend time today thinking about the different ways we "see" Jesus in other forms. When have you seen him lately?

Day 5: John 21:15-19

1. What word or phrase stands out to you from this passage? Why?
2. Why do you think Jesus asked Peter three times if he loved him? How is Peter's life going to change from this point on?
3. Spend time today thinking about whether God is in the driver's seat or passenger's seat of your life. What would change in your life if you gave God total control?

Day 6: John 21:20-25

1. What word or phrase stands out to you from this passage? Why?
2. What is Peter concerned about in these verses? How does Jesus respond?
3. Spend time today thinking about the fact that God has a plan for your life that is different from everyone else's. Are you willing to live it?

Day 7: John 21:1-25

Read through the whole passage and write out the verse that spoke to you the most this week. Meditate on that verse today—and for an extra challenge, memorize it!

From *Studies on the Go* by Laurie Polich. Permission granted to reproduce this page for use in buyer's youth group only. Copyright 2006, Youth Specialties.